Cross-Cultural Interaction in the Novels of Kamala Markandaya

Cross-Cultural Interaction in the Novels of Kamala Markandaya

Md. Irshad

ATLANTIC
PUBLISHERS & DISTRIBUTORS (P) LTD

Published by
ATLANTIC
PUBLISHERS & DISTRIBUTORS (P) LTD
7/22, Ansari Road, Darya Ganj,
New Delhi-110002
Phones : +91-11-40775252, 23273880, 23275880, 23280451
Fax : +91-11-23285873
Web : www.atlanticbooks.com
E-mail : orders@atlanticbooks.com

Branch Office
5, Nallathambi Street, Wallajah Road,
Chennai-600002
Phones : +91-44-64611085, 32413319
E-mail : chennai@atlanticbooks.com

ISBN 978-81-269-1809-6

Printed in India at Nice Printing Press, A-33/3A, Site-IV, Industrial Area, Sahibabad, Ghaziabad, U.P.

Dedicated to

My beloved father
Late Md. Nazim Hassan, Advocate

Foreword

The book entitled *Cross Cultural Interaction in the Novels of Kamala Markandaya* threw me in ecstasy. It will create an indelible impact upon the mind of the readers. The author has given us a comprehensive detail on the subject, which shows his erudition. Md. Irshad, a distinguished Professor of English, is a prolific writer and a prodigious reader. He has contributed a lot to English literature, which we observe in different journals of national repute. He has keen interest in literature and is always engaged in literary activities. His efforts are praiseworthy. English literature is an ocean and we row for novel creation. Prof. Irshad always tries to give us something new which is yet to be explored. I wish him success in life and hope that he continues to present before the readers more books evaluating and analysing the works of well-known English writers.

Dr. Deobrath Prasad Singh, (Akela)
Reader in English,
Nitishwar College, Muzaffarpur

Preface

The present work is an ardent attempt to exhibit how Kamala Markandaya presents in her fictional oeuvre a fine interaction between two varying cultures, indigenous and alien, as complementary to each other, so that the mechanized West may get benefit from the ethical values of India, and the spiritual India profits from the modernization of the West. Kamala Markandaya is a fervent believer in mutual love and understanding. She tries her best to bring together the people of two diverse races and two different attitudes of life. The juxtaposition and interaction of two different civilizations, the Eastern and the Western, are very minutely discussed by the novelist, because her own personality combines in itself the antipodal values of two cultures. She is always in favour of cultural synthesis and compromise between the two ways of life. A peaceful and happy relationship can be developed only by mutual understanding, appreciation and respect. Markandaya claims that the meeting of the twain—the East and the West—is always possible, at least on the personal level. As a keen observer, Markandaya investigates the merits and demerits of both the cultures neutrally.

The book will be useful to the students and teachers of English literature, particularly Indian English literature, and researchers in these fields.

Md. Irshad

Acknowledgements

At the outset, I must acknowledge the impetus and the able guidance given to me by late Dr. P.K. Choudhary, Deptt. of English, B.R.A. Bihar University, Muzaffarpur, for this stupendous task. His patience and labour knew no bounds while guiding and directing me.

I am fortunate in receiving the unstinted help and enthusiastic support of Dr. G.K. Thakur, Prof. & Head, Deptt. of English; and Dr. K.S. Jha, Prof. & former Head, Deptt. of English, B.R.A. Bihar University, Muzaffarpur. My thanks are also due to Dr. Kanupriya, Deptt. of English, B.R.A. Bihar University, Muzaffarpur; Dr. Mamta Rani, Principal M.S. K.B., Muzaffarpur; Dr. R. Nasimi; Dr. S.K. Paul, Deptt. of English, R.D.S. College, Muzaffarpur; Dr. A. Rab Ansari, Deptt. of Hindi, L.S. College, Muzaffarpur; Hon'ble Laxmi Narayan Singh, Secretary; Birendra Kumar Singh, Principal; Prof. Sanjay Chauhan H.O.D. of Zoology; and Dr. Ajay Kumar Singh, H.O.D. of English, N.N. College, Singhara, Vaishali.

I am beholden to my beloved mother, Gulshan Jahan and all the members of my family, friends and Amit Raj, Chairman of Ami Vision, for their strong moral support and help. I express my deepest sense of gratitude to my son Faraz Rashad, my nephews Aman and Babba, my niece Ziya who had always been a reservoir of inspiration at the time of my pursuing the mission. Obviously, I am thankful to Almighty Allah for His inspiration and guidance in all my ventures.

Md. Irshad

Chronology

1924: Born Kamala Purnaiya in Chimakurti, Mysore State, in a Hindu-Brahmin family.

1940: Circa enrolls for B.A. Degree in History at Madras University.

1940-47: Works as a journalist, social worker in village/s.

1948: Leaves for England; gets married to an Englishman.

1954: *Nectar in a Sieve*, London: Putnam; New York: John Day (was Book of the Month selection; translated into at least seventeen languages).

1955: *Some Inner Fury*, London: Putnam; New York: John Day in 1956.

1960: *A Silence of Desire*, Putnam. New York: John Day in 1961.

1963: *Possession*, London: Chatto and Windus. New York: John Day in the same year.

1966: *A Handful of Rice*. New York: John Day.

1969: *The Coffer Dams*. New York: John Day.

1972: *The Nowhere Man*. New York: John Day.

1973: *Two Virgins*.

August 1973: "On Images" at a seminar in socio-literature at the East West Centre for Cultural Exchange, Honolulu.

April 1975: Plenary Speaker at A CLALS conference, Stirling, Scotland; the conference theme was "Commonwealth Writer Overseas."

1976: "One Pair of Eyes: Some Random Reflections" in *Commonwealth Write Overseas*, edited by Alastair Niven.

1977: *The Golden Honeycomb, London*: Chatto & Windus, New York: Thomas Y. Crowell.

1982: Pleasure City. London: Chatto and Windus.

1983: (Titled Shalimar) New York: Harper & Row.

2008: *Bombay Tiger* (Posthumous), New Delhi: Penguin Books India Pvt. Ltd.

Kamala Markandaya passed away on Sunday, May 18, at her home in the outskirts of London in 2004.

Contents

1

Introduction: Culture and Its Dynamic Nature

India is a land of very rich cultural ethos and heritage. Such a marvellous development on the cultural plane is but a result of the influences of Jainism, Buddhism, Islam, Christianity and other religious sects. That is why it is not appropriate to call Indian culture either Hindu or Islamic, either a replica of the Western modes of living and thought or a purely Asiatic product. Some common notions as Truth, Knowledge, Self, the Ultimate Reality and Toleration are the cardinal tenets that form the basis of Indian culture. Despite diversity outwardly there is a pervasive strain of unity inside the cultural life of India. Hence, in the Indian context, culture is undoubtedly a composite whole, a homogenity in which every trait has its definite function, meaning and significance. It has grown up by the assimilation of various features, but it requires the basic conditions as the compatibility of traits, preparedness of the community to receive them, the time factor and others.

As a term, 'culture' is very wide ranging. It has been remarked that "culture is the one thing that we cannot deliberately aim at",[1] since "it is the product of a variety of more or less harmonious activities, each pursued for its own sake".[2] This term has, therefore, different associations as it may be explained with reference to an individual, to a class or a group, or to a whole society. In all situations, there is an element of close inter-relationship between the culture of the individual and that of a group or class, and again between the culture of a group or class and that of the whole society to which that group or class belongs. When one thinks of culture one is led to relate culture to the refinement of manners, to a close acquaintance with the accumulated wisdom of the past, to an interest in manipulating abstract ideas or to the different arts. Often one has all these things in one's mind at the same time. A critic has opined that "it is only by an overlapping and sharing of interests, by participation and mutual appreciation, that the cohesion necessary for culture can obtain".[3]

Culture is indeed an outcome of the blending of two major strands—the native consciousness and the consciousness acquired from alien civilization. The element of adaptability is a must:

> Culture, like a living organism can sustain or etch out a progress only when it shows adaptability to changing situations. The process of evolution, applicable in the case of living species, works equally effectively in the rise and decline of civilization and culture. Indian culture has its adaptability in full abundance.[4]

Only then one perceives the all pervasiveness of integration. Absolutely correct it is to say about culture:

> Integrated pattern of human knowledge, belief, and behaviour that is both a result of and integral to the human capacity for learning and transmitting knowledge to succeeding generations. Culture thus consists of language, ideas, beliefs, customs, taboos, codes, institutions, tools, techniques, works of art, rituals, ceremonies, and symbols. It has played a crucial role in human evolution, allowing human beings to adapt the environment to their own purposes.[5]

Even the remark of Jawaharlal Nehru is very apt:

> There is, I suppose, no culture in the world which is absolutely pristine, pure and unaffected by any other culture. It simply cannot be, just as nobody can say that he belongs one hundred per cent to a particular racial type, because in the course of hundreds and thousands of years unmistakable changes and mixtures have occurred.[6]

To the way of progressive culture, stagnation is a major obstacle, as it prevents the thoughts and ideas from going out or coming in. E.M. Forster observes:

> Culture is a forbidding word. I have to use it, knowing of none better, to describe, the various beautiful and interesting objects which men have made in the past and handed down to us, and which some of us are hoping to hand on.[7]

Culture naturally requires a certain depth. It should be in the possession of dynamic character which is possible when life is faithfully delineated—life that is "essentially dynamic, changing, growing thing".[8] Therefore, culture is ever growing or ever changing along with the flux of time. No doubt, "Whatever stops that dynamic growth injures it and undermines it".[9] Culture may be said to be as the sum of all the forms of art, love, and thought which enabled man to make a progress from time immemorial. It is thus a conglomerate of many elements:

> Does culture mean some inner growth in the man? Of course, it must. Does it mean the way he behaves to others? Certainly it must. Does it mean the capacity to understand the other person? I suppose so. Does it mean the capacity to make yourself understood by the other person? I suppose so. It means all that.... The cultured mind, rooted in itself, should have its windows and doors open. It should have the

> capacity to understand the others' viewpoint fully even though it cannot always agree with it.[10]

Culture and civilization are at most times synonymously used, but both are basically different from each other. Civilization is the organisation of society which creates suitable conditions for culture to flourish; the former refers to the 'outside' of life whereas the latter the 'inside' of life:

> Culture...expresses itself through language and, art, through philosophy and religion, through social habits and customs and through political institutions and economic organizations. No one of them is separately culture but collectively they constitute the expression of life which we describe as culture. Culture is the efflorescence of civilization...here in India culture is almost as extensive as civilization itself.[11]

Hence, civilization may be equated with 'material culture' which includes the tools, weapons, clothing, shelter, machines, etc. while culture is related to the 'non-material' aspect that includes spiritual civilization like language, literature, art, religion, law and government. Explaining the essential ingredients of a cultured civilization, C.E.M. Joad writes:

> Anyway we have discovered some of the things that count as being civilized, making beautiful things, thinking freely and thinking new things, and keeping the rules, without which people couldn't get on together.[12]

As literature is a mirror of life and faithfully gives a 'criticism of life' with a view to interpreting its varied organising strains, so fiction, being a prominent genre of literature, expresses the cultural life of any clime in the best possible way. Indian fiction in English articulates it very meaningfully and effectively. Meenakshi Mukherjee remarks: The definition of 'East' as well as of 'West' varies from novel to novel, but each tries in its own way to grapple with the problem that has continued to concern the Indo-Anglian novelists for more than fifty years. One is struck by the unabating interest shown by these novelists in the interaction of the two sets of values that exist side by side, and often coalesce in the twentieth century.[13]

Its framework in Kamala Markandaya's fictional ouevre is wide as well as various, because the inter-cultural relationship between the East and the West takes "two forms—first direct relationship between Indian and British characters; and secondly the impact of modern urban culture brought in by the British rule on traditional Indian life".[13] So, the forthcoming discussion in different sections of the present work moves around the cross-cultural interaction and assimilation between the indigenous consciousness and the alien one. Kamala Markandaya has very brilliantly explored the essence of cultural assimilation in her novels. The bright aspiration of her characters wants to regenerate and reconstruct a fresh new world of peace and harmony discarding cultural clash. Her extraordinary vision of life has been depicted through her characters. As a true humanist, she has firm faith in cordial human relationships and the universal brotherhood.

NOTES

1. T.S. Eliot, "Conditions of Culture", *Selected Prose*, ed. John Hayward, Penguin, London, 1958, p. 248.
2. *Ibid.*
3. T.S. Eliot, "Definition of Culture" *op. cit.*, p. 247.
4. H.M. Prasad, *Response : Recent Revelations of Indian Fiction in English*, Prakash Book Depot, Bareilly, 1983, p. 30.
5. "Culture", *Britannica Ready Reference Encyclopedia*, Vol. III, New Delhi, p. 88.
6. J.L. Nehru, "What is Culture", *Modern Essays*, Orient Longman, Madras, 2001, p. 121.
7. E.M. Forster, "Does Culture Matter?", *Points of View*, ed. M.A. Pink, Macmillan, New Delhi, 1975, p. 10.
8. J.L. Nehru, "What is Culture", *op. cit.*, p. 122.
9. *Ibid.*
10. *Ibid*, p. 123.

11. Humayun Kabir, "The Unity of Indian Culture", *Prose and Poetry Selections*, Sunrise Publications, Patna, 1996, p. 52.
12. C.E.M. Joad, "A Dialogue on Civilization", *I am the People*, N.C.E.R.T., New Delhi, 2001, p. 72.
13. Meenakshi Mukherjee, *The Twice Born Fiction*, Arnold Heinemann Publishers India Ltd., New Delhi, 1974, p. 65.
14. M.K. Naik, *A History of Indian English Literature*, Sahitya Akademy, New Delhi, 2005, p. 236.

2

Confrontation of Cultures: Indigenous Versus Alien

Cross-cultural interaction is an outstanding feature of Indian writing in English. Novel, the creation of intellectuals, developed in India in the 19th century. The significant outcome of Indo-European contact was the cross-fertilisation between the two very different cultures. Several great novelists like Bankim Chandra Chattopadhyaya, Mirza Q. Baig and Hari Narayan Apte in the latter half of the 19th century were devoted mostly to nationalistic themes—pride and respect for Indian culture and tradition. Many novels were written in the South Indian languages during the colonial period. Many translations of English novels too were produced. The British colonial administrators gave encouragement to 'Vernacular' novelists and got several of their works translated into English. The colonial rulers were eager to get information about regional life, local customs and traditions, since such knowledge was invaluable to them for getting a better grip on governance in India. After the revolt of 1857, the administrators became more aware of Indian sensitivities vis-à-vis their culture and traditions. The new novels contained detailed descriptions of how people dressed, their forms of religious worship, and their many beliefs and practices. Many novelists criticised the social evils present in Indian society and suggested remedies, while others narrated thrilling and adventurous stories of the past. Such glorification of India's past helped in cultivating pride for their cultural heritage among readers.

The way characters spoke in a novel began to indicate their region, class or caste. Novels familiarised readers with the ways in which people in other parts of their land spoke their mother tongues, all the time creating a sense of a shared history and culture. As we know, novels tell imaginary stories but they also describe socio-economic conditions, while the characters are drawn from the society itself. Social novelists created heroes and heroines with ideal qualities, which the readers had no alternative but to admire and try to emulate.

The central dilemma of the colonial novels is: how to remain rooted in the tradition and culture, how to accept Western, i.e. alien but 'modern' ideas, without losing one's identity? The ideal hero successfully blends past with present; he absorbs Western learning and habits, simultaneously following traditional culture and tradition.

As we know that the East and the West first came into contact through trade. But the cultural dislocation took place in the normal lifestyle of the Indians with the introduction of the English language. As S. John Peter Joseph observes:

> Though the Indian mind was thoroughly exposed to the influence of European culture and its ethos, it could not surrender completely to the Western impact. Despite the fact that intellectuals were exposed to the cultural heritage and the political concepts of the west, they only assimilated western values without actually detaching themselves from their indigenous cultural roots.[1]

The sharp distinction has been harmonised by the writers through their organic vision of life. The South Indian writers decided to write in English because at that time the British Empire was at its zenith. They were attracted by the wealth of literature and philosophy of English. At the same time, they were rooted in Indian culture. Obviously, they were bilingual or trilingual. They were equipped with the basic education of Hindu scriptures and folklore; they were conversant with Sanskrit and Tamil classics. A. Madhaviah and K.S. Venkataramani were the voice of social problems and desired to resolve personal conflicts of loyalties and values—East and West, old and new. According to Uma Parameswaran,

> The 'native aliens' were educated in mission schools, they picked up not only more anglicized accents of speech but adopted a more anglicized routine as a way of life. Most of them completed their education outside India. Santha Rama Rau matriculated from St. Paul's school, London; Kamala Markandaya toured Europe before attending Madras University; Balachandra Rajan took his advanced degrees, including his Ph.D., from Cambridge, England. Raja Rao studied in France. Today, all four are expatriates in actuality as they have long been in their writings.[2]

The sense of togetherness is very common in Indian writings:

> Coming of cultures together cannot be a bye-pass phenomenon; it is like the combination of two live wires that run electrical currents.[3]

The assimilation and combination of Western culture with Indian devotion to religion or belief are inexplicable. The class consciousness, the extreme desire for women liberation, stressed self-centredness and proneness to materialism are the results of the influence of the Western culture.

> Cultures at crossroads find a transformation in implied tension, an objective stance in the theme of tradition and change in several significant Indian novelists.[4]

The East stands for passivity, stagnation, rootedness and a kind of conservatism, while the West has a sceptical and pragmatic attitude towards the problems of the world. According to Rekha Jha,

> In the East, Man accepts the forces of nature as invincible...; the West on the other hand, believes that man can strive to master natures

> through the application of science in the form of technology.[5]

The present-day Indian society is the mixture of indigenous tradition and imported Western conception. Obviously, the educated Indians are the product of the conflicts and reconciliations of the dual culture. Allen J. Greenberger observes that "the English writers, likes Rudyard Kipling, believed that there was a basic difference between the East and the West".[6] Without doubt, the West believed in an active positive world, while the East had a passive negative world. The British had confidence in their own culture and they desired to retain their own identity to get success in their endeavour in India. According to their belief, they were Englishmen first and foremost. According to John Masters, they were "like people living in a room upstairs who knew nothing of what was going on in the house below". He points out that the only way was 'to feel India', that you must become Indian; "gain one set of qualities and lose the other".[7] Mrs. Steel felt the need for a "mutual assimilation of East and West without injury to either".[8] Ranga Rao points out:

> An Indian English novelist is a creature of at least two environments: there is his own native ethos within his regional culture; and second the assimilated language milieu. Getting the two to collaborate is the crux of the matter.[9]

The cross-cultural interaction figures prominently in Indo-Anglian novels, particularly those written after independence. The English ruled over India for more than 200 years and there were conflicts and tensions, for Indian patriotism and her pride in her own spiritual culture could not tolerate British domination. The interaction is studied first by Sarath Kumar Ghose in his novel, *The Prince of Destiny*. Raja Rao's *The Serpent and the Rope* protrays the meeting of East and West on the most intimate plane through the story of Rama, an Indian, and Madeleine, a French girl, who meet at a French University shortly after World War II. In fact, the kindred consciousness of the East and the West impinges upon

Ramaswamy's character. The novel is a potent response to the promise or threat of cultural collision. Rekha Jha opines:

> In Raja Rao the East-West theme assumes a depth and validity in the quintessence of the advaita philosophy of Brahmanical India, to the exclusion of India at all other levels. The West is seen as insisting on the particular, the concrete, the personal and the immediate in its recognition of the object as something outside oneself.[10]

Indeed, *The Serpent and the Rope* is a richer piece of fictional art that shows a concern with heritage and heresay. Cultural dualism is felt in blood and bones in Richard Wright, James Baldwin, Ralph Elison, Saul Bellow and Malamud.

Mulk Raj Anand is another major voice in the fictional realm of Indo-Anglian literature. The outstanding theme of his novels has been the cultural interaction of the two modes of life—the Western and the Oriental—and the consequent actuation of the painful process of modernization. The British contact was conducive to the growth of a new angle of vision and in many ways it has been profitable. But cultural pride and feeling of superiority came in the way of harmonious relations. There was the difference of the two irreconcilables: idealism, mysticism and materialism.

In *Coolie*, the East-West theme finds a comprehensive and elaborate treatment. The evils, the injustice and inhumanity of colonial rule have been exposed, and the degradation caused as a result of contact with the West has also been brought out. Anand is one of those Indo-Anglian novelists who are both of the East and West, and who in their novels portray the conflicts and tensions between these two opposite ways of life, and hint at the possible ways of achieving a synthesis of these two contrasted value systems. The British influence as represented in the novel, *Untouchable,* is a force for attitudinal change. It may produce "Pilpali Sahibs" like Bakha and Bashir, contemptuous of their own culture and way of life, but it has also created an 'awakening', a 'consciousness' among the underdogs of society and given a jolt to an outdated and oppressive social system. It has set the Indians on the road to modernity. Obviously, the novels of Mulk Raj Anand are the result of acceptance of Western thinking. He is an ardent believer of modern ideas maintaining a scientific and rational approach to problems and the principle of socialism. His characters are not rootless and unreal. The influence of Marx, Balzac, Tolstoy and Western culture completely coalesces with the visions of Premchand, Tagore, Gandhi and Nehru in his consciousness. In his novels, Mulk Raj Anand articulates his compassion for the victims of so many wrongs and so much misunderstanding. Championing the metaphors of social change, he took upon himself the role of artist as "the conscience of the race, the guide, the mentor".[11] He is the first writer to give Indian novel in English a definite tone and clear texture.

Cross-cultural interaction is also perceptible in the novels of Khuswant Singh. His *Train to Pakistan* is a close analysis of the partition and stands as a milestone in the art of Indian realistic fiction. In *A Bend in the Ganges,* Manohar Malgonkar presents the pre-Independence occurrences and the post-Partition events. The novelist builds up a complex story of criss-cross incidents through a pair of heroes, Devi Dayal and Gian Talwar. The novel is a prism of new ideas, new relations of individual with the society, newer prespectives on people's national awareness, their tension between the decaying and rising values, and the faint contour of the emerging faith of the mutilated multitudes.

Indian fiction in English reflects, like a many-coloured glass, the myriad nuances of tradition and change in Indian life. Indian fiction has rewardingly explored imaginative possibilities of the tension or reciprocation between tradition and change. Prof. M.K. Naik declares:

> ...the modern Indian writer in English is essentially preoccupied with one broad theme, whatever his ostensible subject viz., the theme of the confrontation between tradition and modernity.[12]

R.K. Narayan's novels present a more clear and intrinsic picture of the permanent and transitional values clashing or coalescing together. His fiction reflects the modern India rooted in old traditions and caught up in the crucible change. Malgudi of Narayan is both the matrix of tradition and the crucible change. He is more concerned with translating the East-West dichotomy. In Bhabani Bhattacharya again, the East-West encounter is viewed against "the frail old-world wheel of wood set against the giant machines of the modern age".[13] His novels are the "integration of the simple and the sophisticated; the ancient and the modern; city and village; East and West".[14] Undoubtedly, Indo-Anglian novels presented very clearly "the dynamic changes and attitudes—social, political, intellectual and material—wrought in the Indian social structure by the contact with the West".[15]

In the novels of Nayantara Sahgal, inter-cultural conflict breaks through the facts of inter-cultural tensions. Women characters in her novels have the voltage of rising individuality and surging desires for living a full life. In *A Time to be Happy,* Mira and Rashmi, the mother and daughter, swing towards tradition and change or two phases of culture. In *The Day in Shadow,* Rashmi and Simrit feel that there cannot be such thing as a clean break. The past has its edges that will ever smoothen ones being. Simrit observes that a part of her would always be married to Som. Simrit, symbolic of the Hindu race, representing a culture, a tradition, an enduring passivity, is alien to Som's machine world and different cultural values. Som stands for the cultural values that fail to be coalesced in Indian cultural texture. Raj, on the other hand, is a product of the synthesis of encounters and the union of Simrit and Raj is a hint towards finding a meaning in assimilating without loss to native heritage.

Without doubt the cross-cultural interaction becomes the essential mode of perception in a good number of Indian novels in English. Santha Rama Rau's *Remember the House,* Balchandra Rajan's *The Dark Dancer,* Nayantara Sahgal's *A Time to be Happy* and Raja Rao's *The Serpent and the Rope* are significant novels that render dramatically the tension of identity ensuing from biculturalism. *Remember the House* is a fictional rendering of the dramatic tension in Baba Goray's life.

She returns to India after her education abroad. Both East and West claim on her, making her identity fluid and herself an embryo. The long schooling and varied exciting experiences in the West make her life in India dismal. She feels like meeting the missing element in Alix and Nicky, the American couple, but her attachment does endure. Soon she discovers that all they seem to stand for is a mere mask and their reality is incompatible with her own. The episode of Nicky's kissing her while swimming makes her still more aware of cleavage. Through her marriage with Hari, she comes to accept herself as a real Indian, her roots now firmly planted in Indian culture. Her European education has only intensified her concern for identity enabling her to see herself with emotional sharpness. In her case, the Western experience simply intensifies her dilemma. It does not give her the objectivity to resolve her crisis. She remains in a fix till the end. In Baba Goray's, case, the contrast between cultures makes her restore herself with full understanding and deep emotion. Sanad Shivpal is another variant, a West-educated Indian youth who returns home and is caught up in the dilemma of identity.

> The two worlds, which are juxtaposed in minor characters, representing two sets of values is processed in Sanad's discovery of self. The reality of Western culture on Indian soil is visualised in concrete terms in Sanad's regaining of his roots. Mahatma Gandhi made spinning a crusade against things foreign. In Sanad's case too, it is an act of faith.[16]

Moreover, the choice of the English language to write Indian fiction is central to the cross-cultural interaction. Srinivas Iyengar states:

> ...peculiarities of Indian life and experience and speech...don't easily admit of translation into English terms.[17]

An artistic style has been created very successfully by R.K. Narayan. Raja Rao has also adopted traditional and Puranic modes of narrative. Dr. Rekha Jha remarks:

> India must be presented with its contrasts, paradoxes, ambiguities and contradictions of old and new. The magic of monsoon and the waiting for it in the dust bowl plains; the strangling jungle public worship, poverty and the riches of India, its castes and festivals, the interminable ritual of birth, marriage and cremation in a land where non-violence is preached and violence practised, all these have to be interpreted to an audience unfamiliar with it. The English-language writer also faces the temptation of interpolating such information into his narrative for the benefit of the foreign reader.[18]

The emergence of an entire school of women novelists was a notable development. The remarkable novelists are Ruth Prawer Jhabvala, Kamala Markandaya and Anita Desai. M.K. Bhatnagar opines:

> These writers living a fresh whiff of air—an entirely fresh perspective on the literary scene.[19]

Kamala Markandaya's novels, in comparison with those of her contemporary women writers, seem to be more fully reflective of the awakened feminine sensibility in modern India. She projects the image of the changing Indian traditional society in terms of the growth of the individual consciousness. According to Doireann Macdermott,

> Markandaya has acquired a duality of vision, enabling her to observe both British and Indians with cool detachment...as she herself has said, in spite of being an outsider by choice, 'the eye I see with are still Indian eyes.'[20]

Kamala Markandaya, a very prominent signature of Indian English fiction, was born into an elite Brahmin family, the

Purnaiya of Mysore, in 1924. Martin Tucker, in *Literary Exile in the Twentieth Century*, identifies her place of birth as Chimakurti. She took on the name Markandaya as her literary pseudonym. There was some significance in the choice of that name, so rich with association for the Hindu mind. When Siva asked his devotee, Mrikandu to choose between a dull-witted and unethical son who would live long and one perfect son who would die at sixteen, Mrikandu chose the latter and named him Markandaya. Perhaps she chose the name because the puranic Markandaya went on to live for a very long time with the undiminished energy of a youth. She belonged to an affluent and aristocratic family and got a thoroughly Western upbringing. She was educated at various schools. Her father was in the Indian Civil Service, in the Railways, and this enabled her to travel widely, not only in South India, but also in England and Europe because of 'a pleasant freemasonry' in the railway fraternity. She got admission in the University of Madras for doing graduation in 1940, worked in the Indian Army for some years during the Second World War, and began to work in India as a journalist and writer of short stories. She worked as a proofreader and as a secretary in some private firms. She was awarded the National Association of Independent School Award (U.S.A.) in 1967 and the Asian Prize in 1974. She has been called one of the crispest, and most warmly personal of Indian writers. She married a fellow journalist, Englishman Bertrand Taylor, and permanently emigrated to Britain in 1948. She passed away on Sunday, May 18, at her home in the outskirts of London in 2004. She is survived by one daughter, Kim Oliver, who was with her when she died of kidney failure. In the realm of Indo-Anglian fiction, Kamala Markandaya is held up in high esteem. M.K. Bhatnagar declares:

> She is an impressive explorer of human consciousness and of the convolutions of intimate inter-personal relationships, caught in the whirpool of disparate and divergent cultures.[21]

She has rightly been called an insider-outsider. Shashi Tharoor observes:

> She was a pioneer who influenced all of us Indians writing in English.[22]

She got recognition with the publication of her first novel, *Nectar in a Sieve* (1954) which has been translated into seventeen languages including Russian in 1958.[23] It has been followed by nine other novels. Markandaya had set up a blueprint for herself—to write novels, each of which would depict one stratum of Indian society. Markandaya projects the cultural dilemma of the country in its choice between the stagnant traditional values and ever-moving modernity. Shiv K. Kumar points out:

> The exodus from the villages here symbolises the disinheritance of the human soul, its recantation of the age-old commitment of faith, peace, compassion and truth. Change is, therefore, the focal theme in her novels; it is the pivot around which her fictional world revolves.[24]

The most outstanding feature of Markandaya's fiction is the concept of cultural continuity in the din and bustle of social, economic and political changes in modern India. Markandaya in her novels explores the impact of change in terms of human psychology. For her culture stands essentially for an idea which unites a million individuals and confers on each of them an integral selfhood. Simply, it represents the ideal of "a unitary complex of interacting assumptions, modes of thought, habits and styles, which are connected in secret as well as overt ways with the practical arrangements of a society and which, because they are not brought to consciousness, are unopposed in their influence over men's mind."[25]

Indeed, the novels of Markandaya have an artistic exploration into the human psyche in the context of complex cultural values. This concern for individual consciousness and its growth and refinement is the hallmark of Markandaya's fictional art. Markandaya projects the image of the changing

Indian traditional society in terms of the growth of individual consciousness. Her novels fully explore and delineate in terms of situation and character the "vital, formative areas of individual consciousness that project the image of cultural change".[26] She has shown her acute historical consciousness by treating the tensions and points of contact between people belonging to two different races and two different attitudes of life from various perspectives by bringing them together in different relationships and situations. The West is presented through a number of characters playing different roles, representing different aspects of Western culture, and reacting in different ways to India, its culture and its people they come in contact with. William Walsh further declares:

> Her particular strength lies in the delicate analysis of the relationships of persons specially when there have a more developed consciousness of their problems and are attempting to grope towards some more independent existence. She has been most successful and at her best, an impressive best, in dealing with the problem of the educated and middle class, and she has a gift for delineating the self-imposed laceration of the dissatisfied.[27]

The most striking aspect of Markandaya's worth lies in its examination of the erosion of 'traditional' Indian values by Western 'modernity'. Many of her novels reveal tensions between spirituality and materialism, rural and urban ways of life, rationalism and faith. Markandaya highlighted her own writing as literature of concern. Tradition and change are the outstanding features of her writing. This was a preoccupation with most of the Indo-Anglian fiction until Salman Rushidie's *Grimus* hit the scene in 1975. Her novels deal with the question of identity; her characters are almost always struggling with the 'East-West' clash of codes. As she herself observes, if the East and West have the attitude of compromise they may understand each other. It is supposed that the West has been self-consciously superior and the East self-consciously inferior. Though individual relationship between East and West is feasible, yet political forces may keep barriers in its way. The novels of Markandaya teach us that we should cling to our traditional values, but at the same time we must readily accept what is the best in Western culture. Critics like Fawzia Afzal Khan and David Rubin have drawn a distinction between Markandaya's novels that are set in the Indian context and those that explore inter-racial relationships in either a British or an Indian setting.

Like well-known Indo-English novelists Mulk Raj Anand and R.K. Narayan, Kamala Markandaya accepts the fictional form as a gift of West. Markandaya's works never quite shook off the colonial hangover. This is also true of the style in which she describes the rural urban clash. The violence in her works has always been beneath the surface 'tragic but not grotesque'.

The significant themes of her novels are social, cultural and economic interaction on the cultural plane. Markandaya has been preoccupied with such process of which she herself is a living example. The clash between the Eastern and Western "values lead to an inevitable quest for identity; which she has ably dwelt upon in most of her novels in different contexts and with varying flavour. But she lacks the epic dimension of Raja Rao and the sharp sociological concerns of Mulk Raj Anand who have also dealt with the theme of 'East-West encounter' in some of their novels.[28]

There is a reconciliating harmony in the novels of Kamala Markandaya. She does not approve of the complete merge of Indian culture with the Western one; as such, she is against the elimination of Indian culture through Westernisation. A complete surrender has never been possible nor desirable. Unlike other writers who are of the view that the gap between the East and the West can never be properly bridged, Markandaya seems to suggest that a cultural synthesis and a compromise between the two modes of living are always possible. She tries to establish the point that a harmonious union and lasting relationship between the East and the West can be established only through mutual respect, appreciation and understanding and certainly not through domination.

Normally, national prejudices go against the development of the culture which ought to keep pace with the different cultures of the world. For the development of culture, the door should be kept open for the advent of other creative cultural values. The novelist believes that racialism and fanaticism are stumbling blocks in the way of exchange of cultural values. The former gives birth to violence and bloodshed, whereas the latter creates an atmosphere of hatred and hostility. The foundation of ideal culture is 'Live and Let live' and 'Love the neighbour as thyself'. Cruelty and arrogance are against a civilised culture.

Simply, Kamala Markandaya's characters are educated, well-mannered, and highly sensitive. But all characters are not the same. Hence, uncultured characters have their own class. The main aim of the uncultured is to improve their way of life by coming in contact with the cultured people but in vain. A few of them stand against the traditional way of life. This is an interaction between the two groups—the cultured reform themselves in the light of outside influences, while the uncultured adjust themselves within their own rigid traditional circle. The export and the import of cultural values become obvious through interaction with the British characters; as such, there is a missionary or a British sympathiser in her novels. This cross-cultural interaction is, therefore, an important feature in Kamala Markandaya's novels.

Without any shadow of doubt, Kamala Markandaya has a kind of "mixed sensibility"[29] with which she portrays sensitively and very clearly the clash of the two modes of living —Oriental in cultural traditions and religious heritage and Occidental by habitation. Her deep knowledge and vision of both Eastern and Western values of life provide her an admirable advantage to present the personal, social, political and cultural interactions between the two. Obviously, she is a highly sensitive writer and her authentic delineation of the juxtaposition and interaction of two diverse civilisations, the Eastern and the Western, is a great achievement because her own artistic personality combines in itself the contrary qualities and values of the two cultures.

The present work is, thus, an extremely humble attempt to explicate the process of cross-cultural interaction that is very much evident in the fictional oeuvre of Kamala Markandaya.

NOTES

1. S. John Peter Joseph, "Confrontation and Reconciliation in the Novels of Kamala Markandaya", *Studies in Women Writers in English*, Vol. I, ed. Mohit K. Ray and Rama Kundu, Atlantic Publishers and Distributors, New Delhi, 2004, p. 125.
2. Uma Prameswaran, *Writers of the Indian Diaspora Kamala Markandaya*, Rawat Publications, Jaipur, 2000, p. 17.
3. H.M. Prasad (ed.), *Response: Recent Revelations of Indian Fiction in English*, Prakash Book Depot, Bareilly, 1983, p. 28.
4. *Ibid.*, p. 32.
5. Rekha Jha, *The Novels of Kamala Markandaya and Ruth P. Jhabvala: A Study in East-West Encounter*, Prestige Books, New Delhi, 1990, p. 3.
6. J. Allen Greenberger, *The British Image of India*, London, 1969, p. 30.
7. John Masters, *The Night Runners of Bengal*, New York, 1951.
8. Steel, *The Hosts of the Lord,* N.D., p. 84.
9. Quoted in "From Chatterjee to Chatterjee", *Indian Literature*, No. 144, July-August, 1991, p. 104.
10. Rekha Jha, *op. cit.*
11. H.M. Prasad, *op. cit.*, p. 16.
12. Quoted in H.M. Prasad, *op. cit.*, p. 25.
13. Stephen Hemanway, *The Novel of India*, Vol. II, *The Indo-Anglian Novel,* Writers' Workshop, Calcutta,1975, p. 46.
14. *Ibid.*
15. Milton Singer (ed.), *Introducing Indian Liberal Education*, Chicago, 1957, p. 142.
16. H.M. Prasad, *op. cit.*, p. 36.
17. K.R. Srinivasa Iyengar and Prema Nanda Kumar, *Indian Writing in English*, 4th ed., Sterling, New Delhi, 1984, p. 20.

18. Rekha Jha, *op. cit.*, p. 10.
19. M.K. Bhatnagar, "Kamala Markandaya—the Insider-Outsider", *Kamala Markandaya—A Critical Spectrum*, Atlantic Publishers and Distributors, 2002, p. 1.
20. "Markandaya Kamala (1924) Indian Novelist", *Encyclopeadia of Post-Colonial Literatures in English*, ed. Eugene Beson and L.W. Conolly, Vol. 2, Routledge, London, 1994, p. 986.
21. M.K. Bhatnagar, *op. cit.*, p. 1.
22. Quoted in Suresh Kohli, "Society", *She Took India to the USA,* Online, http://www/boloji.com/wfs252.htm, Accessed on, 4/2/2007, p. 4.
23. Elena J. Kalinnikova, *Indian English Literature: A Perspective*, Vimal Prakashan, Ghaziabad, 1982, p. 150.
24. Shiv K. Kumar, "Tradition and Change in the Novels of Kamala Markandaya", *Osmania Journal of English Studies*, 7, No. 1, 1969, p. 1.
25. Lionel Trilling, *Sincerity and Authenticity,* O.U.P., London, 1972, p. 125.
26. A.V. Krishna Rao, *The Indo-Anglian Novels and the Changing Tradition*, Rao and Raghavan, Mysore, 1972, p. 76.
27. William Walsh, *Commonwealth Literature,* O.U.P., London, 1973, p. 19.
28. Quoted in Bhatnagar (ed.), "The Social Values in the Novels of Kamala Markandaya", *op. cit.*, pp. 156-57.
29. Harish Raizada, "East-West Confrontations in the Novels of Kamala Markandaya", *Perspectives on Kamala Markandaya*, ed. Madhusudan Prasad, Vimal Prakashan, Ghaziabad, 1984, p. 37.

3

A Trilogy on Indian Society

Nectar in a Sieve

Kamala Markandaya's *Nectar in a Sieve*, very much reminiscent of Thomas Hardy's novels, was published in 1954 and made her widely known. It is a relatively short novel that introduces Western people to miserable life in rural India and the changes that occurred during that country's British colonization. Although easy to read, the novel is lyrical and moving and can be read on a variety of levels. On the most basic level, it is the story of an arranged, but loving marriage, and rural peasant life. On another level, it is a tale of indomitable human spirit that overcomes poverty and unending misfortunes. Broadly speaking, it is a novel about the conflicts between a traditional agricultural culture and a burgeoning industrial capitalistic society. The novel touches on several important social phenomena: the importance of traditional cultural practices, people's reluctance to change and the impact of economic change. Finally, it is a story about the resilience of the human spirit and the importance of values.

In this masterpiece of Markandaya, Dr. Kenny represents the West and the tannery stands for modern science, technology and industry. The opposite viewpoints of the East and the West are brought out through the contact of Rukmani and her family with Dr. Kennington though the relations between Rukmani and English doctor seem to be quite friendly, the mutual and the basic inability to perceive and comprehend the motivation and behaviour of each other remains for each of them a common problem.

Dr. Kennington, a cultivated and enlightened British missionary, has been nourished on the noble ideals of liberalism. Obviously, he is a humanitarian; and out of pity for the poverty-stricken and suffering people of India, he has sacrificed his conjugal happiness and pleasures of home for the service of humanity. He serves the rural folk and helps them tirelessly to overcome their miseries. He cures Rukmani and her daughter, Ira, of their barrenness. Later on, he builds a hospital in the village and renders service to people. He seems to be playing two roles. Basically, he is a good foreign missionary whose purpose is to serve the backward people. He is also presented as an observer of life in India and provides the novelist with an opportunity to make an image of the country, as experienced by a sympathetic outsider. He stands for the best outlook of the West. His sense of duty is responded to by Rukmani with her feelings of love, devotion and of worship.

In the beginning, the relationship between Rukmani and Dr. Kennington is one of faith and fear. When she approaches him for his assistance in having a son, she thinks:

> If he wishes to help me he can, so much faith had I in him. My heart was thumping out a prayer.[1]

When Dr. Kennington asks her to come and see him, she becomes afraid. She says:

> My fears came crowding upon me again. I had never been to this kind of doctor; he suddenly became terrifying. (p. 20)

The relationship between Rukmani and the English missionary appeared dubious for the people of the village including the sons and daughter of Rukmani. Though free meetings between men and women are quite natural and common in the Western countries, yet in India such meetings are often looked down upon and censured by the public. Women living in a village regards such kind of meeting very unfair. It is clear with Kunthi's conversation with Rukmani when the latter is on her way back home after her meeting with Dr. Kennington:

> "You keep late hours", Rukmani. "No later than yours", I replied, not liking her tone. "I have my reasons". (p. 59)

Kunti further says:

> Your husband would give much to know where you have been tonight. (p. 60)

The relationship of Rukmani, a native woman, with Kenny, a whiteman, is not in accordance with the Indian moral values. Biswas, the moneylender of the village, is of the opinion that such meeting in immoral. He tells Rukmani: "They say he is a good friend to you" (p. 103). When Rukmani retaliates by saying that Kenny is a benefactor to her family, the moneylender quietly says: "He is also a man" (p. 103).

The relationship of Rukmani with an Englishman is not approved by her children too. Her son Arjun is also dead against her idea of approaching Kenny for getting him a job in the tannery. He boldly remarks:

> Whitemen have power. Indeed they have over men, and events, and especially over women. (p. 52)

Without doubt, Kenny has an immense love and affection for Rukmani and her children. On the other hand, Rukmani has also a great regard for him. Indeed, Kenny and Rukmani are intimate friends and yet their basic cultural difference crops up in their thought, conversation and behaviour. Ambuj Kr. Sharma remarks:

> Her protagonists believe that disillusionment and despair, disappointment and frustration conflict and struggle are the inseparable and integral part of life.[2]

Further, Margaret P. Joseph points out:

> The difference between things as they were, as they are and as they ought to be between the ideal and the actual or between the East and the West.[3]

Kenny's philosophy of life and idea of individualism are quite different from those of Indians. He is absolutely unable to understand fatalism. He often speaks to them in harsh words, but it is obvious that his harsh words are in themselves an expression of his deep and pure love for them. He has a firm belief that one should fight for a better condition of life. When Rukmani declares her hope that time will be better, he immediately reacts:

> Times are better, times are better. Times will not be better for many months. Meanwhile you will suffer and die, you meek suffering fools. Why do you keep this ghastly silence? Why do you not demand—cry out for help—do something? There is nothing in this country, oh God, there is nothing. (p. 44)

Once again he says when he looks at agony and pain of the poor:

> You must cry if you want help. It is no use whatsoever to suffer in silence. Who will succor the drowning man if he does not clamour for his life? (p. 113)

The wide gap between the Oriental and the Occidental modes of living becomes vivid and crystal clear in the conversation between Rukmani and Kenny. Kenny scornfully says:

> ...do you think spiritual grace comes from being in want, or from suffering? What thoughts have you when your belly is empty or your body is sick? Tell me they are noble ones and I will call you a liar. (p. 114)

Rukmani tries to explain her point clearly:

> Yet our priest fast, and inflict on themselves severe punishments, and we are taught to bear our sorrows in silence, and all this is so that the soul may be cleansed. (p. 114)

When he listens to her argument, he replies:

> My God! I do not understand you. I never will. Go before I too am entangled in your philosophies. (p. 114)

The author has juxtaposed Rukmani and Kenny as representatives of Oriental and Western cultures and traditions respectively. Kenny, according to K.R. Chandrasekharan, "...has the dual role of sympathetic observer of the Indian scene and representative of the finer traditions of the West."[4]

Observing this it is evident that the relationship between the East and the West is not based upon understanding. Friendship, understanding and companionship between the East and the West are possible at the personal level, but the people in India generally find a no-man's land between themselves and the Englishmen. The bond of spiritual love binds Britain and India in the friendly relationship between Kenny and Rukmani. Markandaya's present novel, also subtitled as *A Novel of Rural India*, is a realistic document of a village assaulted by industrialization. She through her heroine, Rukmani, presents a powerful criticism of industrialization and its intrusion upon the placid rhythm and calm beauty of the village. The encroachment of industry causes the decay of natural beauty, creates havoc in village economy, uproots a tenant farmer, brings in social degradation and the loss of traditional and human values. The construction of tannery is a symbol of change. It is a sign of modernity. It is from the very beginning that Rukmani opposed its establishment. It spoils the natural beauty by din and bustle, filth and dirt:

> Already my children hold their nose when they go by, and all is shouting and disturbance and crowd wherever you go. Even the birds have forgotten to sing, or else their call is lost to us. (p. 29)

The past is very vividly compared with the present by the heroine, Rukmani:

> At one time there had been kingfishers here flashing between the young shoots for our fish,

> and paddy birds, and sometimes in the shallower reaches of the rivers, flamingoes, striding with ungainly precision among the water reeds, with plumage of a glory not of this earth. Now birds came no more, for the tannery lay close—except crows and kites. (p. 39)

Simply, Rukmani is not against change but she is against a sudden change and the loss of social values. She says:

> But the change that came into my life, into all our lives, blasting its way in our village seemed wrought in a twinkling of a second. (pp. 27-28)

She is in extreme pain for the social degradation and moral debasement:

> They had invaded our village with clatter and din had taken from us the 'maidan' where our children played, and had made the bazaar prices too high for us. (pp. 27-28)

Rukmani considers this urbanisation as a tragedy. She regards tannery as the key to all her troubles:

> None but these would have laid hands on her (Ira). My sons had left because it frowned on them, one of them had been destroyed by its ruthlessness. (p. 134)

Markandaya's concern is with the traditional life of an Indian village in transition. The construction of a tannery changes the face of the village and alters the lives of its inhabitants 'in a myriad ways' (p. 135).

Like K.S. Venkataramani's *Murugan the Tiller* (1927), Markandaya presents the character of an Indian peasant in an atmosphere of changing economic scenerio. The cultural dilemma of the country in its choice between the stagnant old traditional values and modernity is very much explicit in this novel. The old order is just giving place to the new order. This change is effectively highlighted by Shiv K. Kumar:

> The exodus from the villages here symbolises the disinheritance of the human soul, its

> recantation of the age-old commitment to faith, peace, compassion and truth. Change is, therefore, the focal theme in her novels; it is the pivot round which her fictional world revolves.[5]

Rukmani, the protagonist, becomes the victim of change. As A.V. Krishna Rao observes:

> Spiritual stamina of Rukmani against such formidable enemies to her culture: the draconian landlord and the soulless industry.[6]

No doubt, she is a rebel against change, against industrialization, against the disappearance of the old landscape. Further, she has been called "steady traditionalist" (Rao, p. 66). The consciousness of change is reflected in her novel as one discovers in the fictional works of Mulk Raj Anand, R.K. Narayan and Raja Rao. Here, we are reminded of Hardy's Wessex novels, where the agrarian communities are displaced by the new industrial society. Obviously, the novel dramatises the disruption of a Hindu joint family of farmers owing to industrialization.

Indeed, cultivation, a major occupation in the village, has received a great setback with the introduction of industrialization. The clash between agriculture and industry is introduced in the novel through the setting up of a government tannery in the village. Some of the villagers were ready to accept the new trends of industrialization, but they are strongly opposed by Rukmani:

> "Never, never", I cried "they (the owners of the tannery) may live in our midst but I can never accept them, for they lay their hands upon us and we are all turned from tilling to barter, and hoard our silver since we cannot spend it, and see our children go without the food that their children gorge, and it is only in the hope that one day things will be as they were that we had done these things." (p. 28)

Rukmani represents the spirit of tradition and she is pained to see Kunti, Kali, Janaki and Nathan accepting the change—the tannery and the present. She utters:

> So they were reconciled and threw the past away with both hands so that they may be readier to grasp the present, while I stood in pain, envying such easy reconciliation and clutching in my own two hands the memory of the past, and accounting it a treasure. (p. 29)

She, too, was reconciled when her two sons, Arjuna and Thambi, joined the tannery. She had to realise the hard fact that the land was not enough to accommodate all her sons. The growth of industrialization has been rendered through Rukmani's statement:

> It was a great sprawling growth, this tannery. It grew and flourished and spread. Not a month went by but somebody's land was swallowed up, another building appeared. Night and day the tanning went on. A never ending line of carts brought the raw material in.... The officials of the tannery had increased as well. Apart from the whiteman we had first seen who owned the tennary and lived by himself—there were some nine or ten Muslims under him. They formed a little colony of their own...they were a queer lot, and their way of life was quite different from ours. (p. 47)

Tannery became the symbol of immorality and exploitation and Rukmani's intuitive perception was becoming true. Her daughter, Ira, who had been sent back by her husband for being unable to bear a child for him, took to prostitution in the tannery colony in her despicable attempt to save her child brother, Kuti, from starvation. For demanding more wages, Arjun and Thamby were dismissed by the authority of the tannery. And her fourth son Raja, was brutally killed by the tannery's watchman, allegedly for crossing the boundary wall and stealing one calf skin. Two persons on behalf of the authority came to Rukmani to ensure that

Rukmani and Nathan should not demand any compensation for Raja's death. The contrast between the amoral world represented by the tannery and the simple innocent world of the peasants, comes up in the following conversation:

> Compensation, I thought, what compensation is there for death? I felt confused, I did not understand what he was getting at.... "The point is", the other said, and he thumped on the floor to emphasise his point "that no fault attaches to us. Absolutely one...it is your loss, but not our responsibility.... (pp. 91-92)

No doubt, Rukmani's innocent question is the voiceless agony of millions of mother. She is bewildered with the statement of the tannery manager. The greed, shrewdness and inhumanity of the industrialists are depicted very ironically. Ramesh K. Srivastava points out:

> The tannery represents a world of immorality, greed and corruption invading another which is moral, happy and pure.[7]

The final blow from tannery was the requisition of the land that Nathan had taken on rent from landlord. Rukmani's apprehension that the tannery would eventually be their undoing, comes true:

> I had known it since the day the carts had come with their loads of bricks and noisy dusty men, staining the clear soft greens that had once coloured our village and clearing its cool silence with clamour. Since then it had spread like weeds in an untended garden, strangling whatever life grew in its way. (pp. 133-34)

Simply, Rukmani's hopes, aspirations and the memory of her simple joy had disapeared. Her two eldest sons had already gone to Ceylon, after being sacked. Her daughter gave birth to an illegitimate son, Sukrabani, and Rukmani herself had to leave the hut which her husband had built for her with his own hands:

> This hut with all its memories was to be taken from us, for it stood on land that belonged to another. And the land itself by which we lived. It is a cruel thing, I thought. They do not know what they do to us. (p. 135)

Uprootedness is an outstanding feature of this novel besides poverty, hunger and exploitation. Rukmani and Nathan became part of the land that they cultivated and parting from the land means uprooting the souls. The connection of 'self' and 'place' is obvious here and the crisis of identity is clear. Rootedness as well as helplessness is visible in the character of Nathan.

> In the city, he loses his hold and progressively deteriorates in physical and mental strength. He feels quite uprooted; he can no longer survive. Rootedness in Markandaya is related to the theme of personal freedom in the context of social and communal responsibility. The secret of survival is one's rootedness in one's cultural tradition in a fast changing society.[8]

Mira in *Some Inner Fury*, Helen in *The Coffer Dams* and Saroja in *Two Virgins* do not bid goodbye to their roots. Similarly, Rukmani derives her sustenance from her love for roots. Nathan's roots are in his land and one is torn apart when divorced from the land. This power of rootedness is also traceable in the novels of B. Rajan's *Dark Dancer* and Raja Rao's *The Serpent and the Rope*. Of course, the land is the symbol of hope, and also responsibility. Rukmani, a heroic figure, utters when she enters her native village:

> I looked about me at the land and it was life to my starving spirit. I felt the earth beneath my feet and wept for happiness. (p. 189)

Pearl S. Buck in her novel *The Good Earth* describes the same spirit. The land is life-blood to the Chinese peasant, as to the Indian. Further, the land in *Nectar in a Sieve* is opposed to the symbol of wildness and wilderness of the city. The advent of industrialization has destroyed the traditional agrarian set of values in this novel. Although the novel concludes on a positive "note of quiet strength and resolution."[9]

Moreover, the crisis of culture is very openly presented by the novelist. The difference between a Hindu woman's approach to marriage and that of a woman in foreign countries is mirrored in this conversation between Rukmani and Kenny:

> What then if his wife cannot accompany him? "Cannot?", I said, "she must. A woman's place is with her husband". He sighed impatiently. "You simplify everything, being without understanding. Your views are so limited it is impossible to explain to you." "Limited, yes", I agree. "Yet not wholly without understanding. Our ways are not your ways. (p. 108)

Due to the changing times, the wedding of Rukmani was not half as colourful as her three sisters' had been. The power and prestige of her father has gone. Changes in agrarian politics and economics made him unable to fulfil the demands of exorbitant dowry. The following paragraph is "a sociological commentary of the changing times."[10]

> Shanta first, a big wedding that lasted for many days, plenty of gifts and feasts, diamond earrings a gold necklace, as befitted the daughter of the village headman. Padmini next, and she too made a good match and was married fittingly, taking jewellery and dowry with her; but when it came to Thangam, only relations from our own village came to the wedding and not from surrounding districts as they had done before, and the only jewel she had was a diamond nose-screw. (pp. 1-2)

Francis C. Assisi opines:

> The novel, published less than a decade after India won its independence from Britain, is clearly influenced by this event, portraying some of the problems encountered by the Indian people as they dealt with the changing

> times,...some of the struggles that the main character, Rukmani, faces are the result of the changing times, but they are the kinds of struggles (poverty, death, loss of tradition) that are experienced by many people for many reasons.[11]

Shiv K. Kumar comments on the interplay of tradition and change in her art:

> What distinguishes her most intensively from other Indian novelists is her acute awarness of shift in values that has been taking place in this subcontinent during the past two decades or so.[12]

Thus, this maiden venture of Kamala Markandaya presents the realistic picture of the Indian society. Markandaya unfolds the cultural confrontation and assimilation of the East and the West very realistically. The weakness and strength of both cultures are highlighted here.

Some Inner Fury

The second outstanding novel of Markandaya, *Some Inner Fury,* focuses on a totally different aspect of life—the painful ordeal of the struggle for India's independence. The whole novel revolves round the unforgettable year of 1942, when the clash between the East and the West changed history, not only of nations but also of individuals.

The novel presents very vividly the romantic infatuation between an Indian girl Mira and a British official Richard Marlowe against the backdrop of the Quit India Movement. Without doubt, it is a novel of love, a love between two individuals of different races, of the ruling and the ruled classes, and consequently there is a deep impact of the troubled national spirit of the early forties upon their love. Mira, the heroine, is caught in the whirlpool of nationalist politics. She is in an awkward dilemma to choose either love or the Indian cause. She was on the one hand absolutely unable to close her eyes to the political reality and on the other to renounce her passionate love for Richard, the guide and guardian of her heart and soul. Their story presents the cultural conflict very sharply. Here Markandaya succeeds in blending the love story with the more fundamental issues.

Obviously, they represent two nations. Mira, unknown to the racial difference, is willing to take her side with her people. Circumstances forced her to realise that she cannot detach herself entirely from the conflicting social forces. The crisis of Mira shows affiliations, association, loyalties and responsibilities.

Richard, the hero, a creature of God,[13] is a dashing personality having "the skin as tight and firm as a silken sheath. A body that might have been sculptured though not from marble, hard and smooth, lean, flanked, its lines and surfaces clear cut, unflawed and a warmth to it—such a warmth that could wrap you about gently or make you melt, or set you on fire and burn with an incandescent heat itself" (p. 197). The attractive personality of Richard compels Mira and she falls in love with him at first sight. Very unconsciously, she garlands Richard instead of Kit on their arrival from England. Furthermore, Richard is liberal, sensitive and sympathetic. Chandrasekharan opines:

> Kamala Markandaya has warm appreciation of the Englishman as an individual, he is a gentleman to the core and is free from any feeling of racial superiority.[14]

He is ever ready to take in the new experiences of landscape and culture. He loves the long walks he and Mira take; he hates commercialism and loves beauty, as seen in his act of throwing away the plastic goddess and sending an artistically wrought ivory image of the same, goddess as a birthday gift; he is uninhabited and non-judgemental about the world he sees around him. He gets bored with the all-British parties to which he is invited, and he tries out all kinds of restaurants, including one where he sits on the floor, further he is 'well-versed in the Hindu epics' (p. 145).

This novel is very close to *A Passage to India* of E.M. Forster. The final messages are the same: East and West cannot meet; the time is not yet ripe. As in Forster, characters represent more than themselves, carrying the weight of their race and colonial identity.

But the Indo-British connection seems to have overcome all barriers of race and culture to emerge as a composite identity during the Quit India Movement. Bhupal Singh points out:

> In the days of Clive and Warren Hastings, when Englishmen in India were not so numerous as now, and when many Englishmen who came to India did not hope to return to their motherland, it was not uncommon for Englishmen to marry Indian girls. There was little prejudice against such marriage and there is no suggestion in any novel that such marriages were unhappy.[15]

Without doubt, Kit and Govind, the two cousins, represent different attitudes of the Indians. Kit is a Westernized Indian whereas Govind dislikes the British and is a true Indian by nature. There is a conflict between Kit and Premula as the latter is the worshipper of Indian culture while Richard, an Englishman, is loved by Kit's sister, Mira. Richard respects all cultures and is a passionate lover of East-West harmony, while Mira has a bitter hatred for the Britishers. She remarks at joining the political agitators:

> Go? Leave the man I loved to go with these people? What did they mean to me, What could they mean, more than the man I loved? They were my people those other were his. Did it mean something then all this 'Your people' and my people...? For us there was no other way, the forces that pulled us apart were too strong. (p. 243)

But Richard has no parochial consideration of 'your people and my people' (p. 138).

> Racial and cultural differences do not in any way interfere in the novel with happy sex and love relations. The minds of Mira and Richard

> work in perfect unison and they are able to establish positive relationship at these levels.[16]

Richard's liberality and adaptability are noticed when he and Mira go to a Brahmin restaurant and Richard takes off his shoes and sits on the floor like everyone else as if he had been used to it all his life. Mira bursts:

> There is no one at all like my love. (p. 45)

Furthermore, in his curiosity to appreciate India and its culture, he has also learnt many stories from the *Mahabharata*. The East-West confrontation is highlighted here:

> The house itself was equipped to cope with both Europeans and Indians; there were two Dining Rooms, two pitches, even two sets of servants, the one lot knowing Indian cookery and service, the other trained by Europeans. (p. 29)

The conflict between the two cultures is on the personal level in the case of Mira, like B. Rajan's Krishnan in *Dark Dancer* (1958) and Nalini in *Too Long in the West* (1961):

> The clash of two races, the one grinding with its heel the other, had gone on for a long time. There comes a time when the subordinate race would no more be subordinate, and though there occur individual friendships between members of the two races, the racial difference would not end.[17]

The theme of alienation is also highlighted in the novel, *Some Inner Fury*. Mira decides to violate the rigid social codes of conduct to get 'freedom of a culture in transition'.[18] She desires to accompany Richard on a holiday and loses contact with her mother. She wants to live in the state of freedom forever. She is in search of an identity in changing milieu. She had renounced security for freedom:

> I had left it of my own choice and had no wish to rescind the decision. Yet there were times.... (p. 113)

She has beaten the untrodden path of her own free will, in search of freedom, and now restless, she craves for her identity. She has indulged her own will in seeking freedom and hence is restless when external forces become powerful. She, along with Richard, tries hard to preserve a relationship based on mutual love and trust. Again she finds that unknown forces erect unseen walls between them slowly. As H.M. Williams says, they realise about their success by asserting "the claims of individual human nature and passionate love against the claim of race politics and family."[19] But the deaths of Kit and Premala and the trial of Govind evoke the sense of hatred and finally Mira and Richard got separated. Mira declares:

> I thought there was no region of my mind I could not enter if I tried. I did not know—I had yet to learn—that no man knows himself. (p. 138)

Further Mira says that she could live like that forever and Richard replies:

> I feel I could too; at this moment I'm certain I could. But you know, I don't think one can keep the world at bay for a life time. (p. 191)

Hence, the marrige between an Indian woman and an Englishman is not possible because they belong to two peoples and two cultures which are too different to realise or compromise. One is reminded here of *Esmond in India* of Jhabvala. Mira returns to her culture and accepts her responsibility to her society. She utters:

> And yet it was our life, by our own choice, by being born when we were, even if one were so minded, by destiny. We created it, as much as it created us; belonged to it as much. This other living, so briefly ours, was an escape, an interlude, set in a definite limited span of time.... To keep our peace we would have to go back then to the world from which we came, to which we would always return because it was a part of us even as the earth was of these others who stayed. (p. 192)

In the character of Markandaya, rootedness in culture is of prime importance. There is no survival without roots. Because of her rootedness, Mira gets the verdict of the political and historical reality. Srinivas does not survive without roots. Helen and Bashiam hunt up new roots. Kenny tries to establish roots in an alien country.

The emotions of Mira and Richard are neither crushed nor destroyed. Mira goes ahead though painfully to a higher level of perception, to maturity. In this way, she remembers the good along with the bad. According to Shirwadkar,

> Mira is not defeated in the pursuit of physical, mental and emotional freedom, but she learns that there are many dimensions to freedom.[20]

About the personal relationship, Ramesh Chadha declares:

> Personal attraction coupled with genuine open mindedness to each other's people and culture brings them close to each other on the personal level, but politically and culturally, no nation can tolerate the domination of the other. The passions and aspiration of an individual are sacrificed for a larger cause.[21]

In short, we can say that in this novel Markandaya has portrayed the East-West relationship in a man-woman context like *Possession* and the *Nowhere Man*. Being an Indian, she values Indian traditions and culture more them those of the West.

A Silence of Desire

Markandaya in her third novel, *A Silence of Desire,* presents very brilliantly the psychological maladjustment of a married couple of an urban middle-class family. The feud has cropped up due to conflict of sensibilities based on tradition-modernity contrast.

The relation between Dandekar and his wife Sarojini is badly affected as there is a huge gap between their beliefs—spiritual versus rational. Their socio-cultural tradition provokes the situation, creating a serious breach in communication. The relationship of two individuals is focused in this novel on the basis of matrimony and the 'lack of contact'[22] in the absence of understanding. The novel is based on the life of a middle-class family having a husband, a wife and three minor children in a metropolitan town in South India. Dandekar, a senior clerk in a central government office, is happy with his family. His wife, Sarojini, is very managing and caring. She discharges her marital responsibilities very well. Suddenly, after fifteen years of married life, Dandekar begins to doubt Sarojini's fidelity. The reason for this doubt is that she has started to visit a Swami, known as faith-healer. She begins to go to the Swami because she has a growth in her womb and, therefore, she hopes that the Swamy will cure her of it. In the beginning, she would like to hide her visit from her husband. But Dandekar suspected her faithfulness and thinks that some other man now has her affections. He spies on her movements and one day he caught her sitting before the Swamy:

> She was sitting, cross-legged, on the man's [the Swamy's] right. His hand was on her bowed head, and he was murmuring to her, his voice sometimes falling to a whisper, a soft stream of indistinguishable words. In a rough circle about them sat a small group of men and women, listening—so engrossed that no one turned as he [Dandeker] burst in.[23]

The reason for discord is very sharp here as there are two different views of Dandekar and Sarojini. Sarojini has an unreasoned faith in the healing power of the Swamy and Dandekar has an extreme rational belief. Edwin Thumboo has rightly said:

> Markandaya is too mature to give a 'bold disquisition' on the conflict between faith and reason.[24]

As the novel proceeds, Sarojini realises to go ahead to face reality and Dandekar observes that there are realms of experience which he can never understand well. In short, it can be said that the Swamy proves himself as a silent agent for their lessons. Consequently, the need of understanding in human relations echoes in almost all the novels of Markandaya.

Dandekar, an alien to both British and Indian cultures, is the product of the effect of British culture and education. Thus, he is a rootless fellow. He feels content as long as his wife preserves his domestic security and does not hamper his professional life. He has given her place as she is a conventionally responsible wife. Dandekar is called: "part-eastern and part-western mind" (p. 3). He accepts the tradition of his own beloved culture as it ensures security and a deep sense of belonging. He believes in the cultural-pattern of the faithful, obedient wife and dominant husband and when this is threatened, he is shattered.

The compromise between personal freedom and domestic responsibility is also visible in this novel. Dandekar, being partly Westernised, cannot accept the reality of a faith healing Swamy. On the other hand, he does not provide freedom to Sarojini to visit either a Swamy or a lover. It shows the rootedness in Eastern tradition. Hence, he would like to dominate over his wife. He is dead against the personal choice of his wife, though she is always ready to discharge her marital responsibility. Dandekar is indignant, when she assumes the freedom to choose. The absence of Sarojini makes him disturbed and doubtful. She tells a lie when he asks for the trunk key. She says that she does not know where it is because "she had taken it out to oil the rust out of it" (p. 34).

And indeed, "it has been oiled when he finds it in the keychain" (p.38). Uma Prameshwaram quotes:

> She figures out that he has seen the photograph and preempts his query, as it were, saying she had a photograph of her music teacher; but by now, Dandekar's antennae have been up.[25]

Dandekar utters: "Why had Sarojini lied? Had she? Was she playing some matrimonial game? Was it conceivable, feasible, that she might" (p. 43).

The life of Dandekar was contented, peaceful, his home quiet, and Sarojini served him hot meal. But he was compelled to have a cold meal in the frequent absences of Sarojini from home. He had "...never cooked a meal, never fried a chilly or a potato. Men never did, unless they were cooks and even cooks wouldn't cook in their own homes" (p. 139).

The effect of the visit of Sarojini to the Swamy to whom she confesses to be going to get cured of a painful growth in her womb by faith and prayer, results in his growing "withdrawn, questioning, introspective" (p. 98). And his house shows his intense sorrow:

> ...the place seemed pale and chill, like an unlit lamp." (p. 77)

He points out that the Tulsi plant which his wife worships with great devotion is merely "a plant; one did not worship plants" (p. 5).

Markandaya would like to convey that there should be a complete harmony and proper understanding in husband-wife relationship. Suspicion without proof is the greatest enemy of conjugal harmony. It is obvious that in the beginning of the novel Dandekar shows an unflinching faith in Sarojini:

> She was a good wife, Sarojini good with the children, an excellent cook, an efficient manager of his household, a woman who still gave him pleasure after fifteen years of marriage less from the warmth of her response than from her unfailing acquiescence to his demands. He was lucky.... (p. 14)

But suspicion in the mind of Dandekar takes place with the faith of Sarojini in Swamy. He realises "the pattern of his life being twisted out of shape" (p. 77). At this acute crisis, he is in dire need of advice from his bosom colleague Sastri. He would like to set things right. His tireless efforts to talk some sense into Sarojini's head and his pitiable pleading with the Swamy to dissuade her from visiting him end up in a fiasco. Hence, he finds himself fighting with 'something invisible' (p. 170). His mind becomes restless with unanswerable questions:

> Questions, questions, questions, Dandekar's knuckles dug into his forehead. They crowd into my brain and it's like you (Sastri) said, I

> don't know the answers. I suppose it's because I've never had to think much about anything until now, but I don't seem able to think straight, do anything. All I know is I can't go on like this. (p. 171)

Rajan was cured by the Swamy and it gives a shock to him further. Sarojini informs him:

> I do not expect you to understand. You with your Western notions, your superior talk of ignorance and superstition when all it means is that you don't know what lies beyond reason and you prefer not to find out. (p. 35)

Sarojini feels better everytime she goes there. She is well aware that the pain is still there but it does not touch her in the presence of Swamy. Here she gets relief from the pain born of a sense of neglect and worthlessness. M. Rajeshwar has observed:

> Her neurotic need for love and self-importance are amply attended to by him. It produces a temporary euphoria which neutralizes the physical pain for the time being. Before Sarojini knows it, the Swamy's image is internalized and going to him becomes something of an addition.[26]

She, simply, could not understand the distinction between the needs of her body and psyche. Therefore, she falls into a false belief that "Without faith I shall not be healed" (p. 87). On the one hand, Sarojini is happy in her pain while Dandekar is tortured. Sarojini's deep and individual involvement with Swamy is implicit and unquestioning. She believes that his touch upon her head will dissolve the tumour in her womb. She is strengthened with his look, his smile and his word. She behaves like a woman who is carrying on a passionate liaison. She continues her visits to the Swamy and her household affairs as well as her three children suffer neglect. Dandekar himself, who has been dutiful office clerk, now cannot put his heart and soul in his work, with the result that his work is neglected and runs into heavy arrears. Ghosh, the unsympathetic North Indian officer in charge during the absence of the permanent boss Chari who was on leave, threatens Dandekar with dismissal. The happy family faces financial crisis also. The family is on the verge of collapse. Out of sheer frustration, Dandekar starts visiting prostitutes. He tries his best to wrest Sarojini back from the Swamy's orbit of influence. He visits the Swamy to his village retreat and pleads with him to refuse to see her, but Swamy does not make the desired promise and Sarojini's visits continue. Dandekar tells the Swamy that Sarojini "gives and gives" and that he does not stop her. The Swamy answers:

> If I were to compel her not to give I would also be free to compel her to give. That is the other face of the coin, the other half of what you ask. Can you not see it? (p. 155)

Dandekar falls seriously ill. The situation is nerve-racking indeed. But after the illness Dandekar makes up his mind and launches the final assault on the Swamy. He tells everything to his sympathetic South Indian boss, Chari, and seeks his help in the matter. Consequently, Swamy becomes a controversial figure and so he decides to leave the town. He goes but nobody knows where. He releases Sarojini, advising her to go to hospital for the treatment and the family's ruination is averted. The Swamy has taught Sarojini the lesson of freedom from all bonds.

Dandekar becomes aware of Sarojini's decreasing sense of responsibility and it is very critical when he notices the pitiable condition of his beloved daughter Ramabai. His own sense of responsibility emerges strongest in relation to his children. He proceeds to develop a fullness of relationship with Sarojini. He realises the value for others and can now accept the different sides of life including the traditional and the modern. He declares:

> I didn't know what I was doing and 'I wanted—so little. My wife—I wanted her back, that was all. (p. 223)

He realises well that his silver cups and gold chains are useless before his wife. The two weeks of his illness sensitise him to the suffering of Sarojini and sober him. He is not sexually attracted towards her. He now looks at her "from another aspect of love" (p. 191) and notices "the flesh flower pale and beautiful under the thin blue cotton she wore without desire" (p. 191). He would like to get her back, "not merely because he desired her", but because of "a spiritual ingrowing which made it impossible for him to be whole so long as any part of her was missing" (p. 191). The changed attitude of Dandekar is like a night storm which is followed by a gentle drizzle in the morning.

Towards the end of the novel, both Dandekar and Sarojini make a compromise. Both return to a sense of responsibility towards the family and to the realisation of the rights of others.

In short, the elements of cultural assimilation is evident in *Nectar in a Sieve, Some Inner Fury* and *A Silence of Desire.* Markandaya tries to uphold the concept of a happy global world depicting unity in diversity. She would like to bridge the gap between the two divergent modes of living by the virtues of trust, tolerance, compassion and responsibility.

NOTES

1. Kamala Markandaya, *Nectar in a Sieve*, Jaico Publising House, Mumbai, 2003, p. 20.

   (All subsequent references are to this addition and the page numbers are given at the end of the quotations in parentheses.)
2. M.K. Bhatnagar, *Kamala Markandaya: A Critical Spectrum*, Atlantic Publishers and Distributors, New Delhi, 2002, p. 188.
3. P. Margaret Joseph, *Kamala Markandaya*, Arnold Heineman, New Delhi, 1980, p. 211.
4. R.K. Chandrasekharan, "East and West in the Novels of Kamala Markandaya", *Critical Essays on Indian Writing in English* (ed.), M.K. Naik, S.K. Desai, G.S. Amur, Macmillan, India, 1977, p. 320.
5. Shiv K. Kumar (ed.), "Tradition and Change in the Novels of Kamala Markandaya", *Osmania Journal of English Studies*, 7, No. 1, 1969, pp. 1-10.

6. A.V. Krishna Rao, *The Indo-Anglian and the Changing Tradition, A Study of the Novels of Kamala Markandaya, Anand, R.K. Narayan, R. Rao*, 1930-65, Rao and Raghavan, Mysore, 1972, p. 57.
7. *Six Indian Novelists in English,* Guru Nanak Dev University Press, Amritsar, 1987, p. 116.
8. A.V. Krishna Rao, Madhavi K. Menon, *Kamala Markandaya, A Critical Study of Her Novels*, B.K. Publishing Corporation, New Delhi, 1997, p. 22.
9. M.K. Naik, *op. cit.*, p. 73.
10. Uma Parameswaran, *Kamala Markandaya—Writers of the Indian Diaspora*, Rawat Publication, Jaipur, 2000, p. 58.
11. Francis C. Assisi, "Homage to Kamala Markandaya",

    Online: *http:* www.beilharz.com/authors/markandaya, Accessed on 3/31/2007.
12. Shiv K. Kumar, *Osmania Journal of English Studies*, 1969, pp. 6-11.
13. Kamala Markandaya, *Some Inner Fury,* Putnam, London, 1955, p. 196.

    (All subsquent references are to this addition and the page numbers are given at the end of the quotations in parentheses.)
14. M.K. Naik, *op. cit.*, p. 320.
15. Bhupal Singh, *A Survey of Anglo Indian Fiction*, Curzon Press, London, 1934, p. 165.
16. S. Krisnamorthy, A. Rashmi. *Indo English Fictional Experiments with Inter Racial and Inter Cultural Relationship*, Alien Voice, ed. A.K. Srivastava, Print House, Lucknow, 1981, p. 90.
17. A.V. Krishna Rao, *op. cit.*, p. 35.
18. John F. Adkins, "Kamala Markandaya: Indo-Anglian Conflict as Unity", *Journal of S. Asian Literature*, 10, 1, Fall 1974, p. 95.
19. H.M. Williams, *Studies in Modern India Fiction in English*, Vol. 2, Writers Workshop, Calcutta, p. 169.
20. Meena Shirwadkar, *Image of Women in the Indo-Anglian Novels*, Sterling, New Delhi, 1979, p. 38.

21. Remesh Chadha, "Cross-Cultural Interaction in Indian English Fiction", *An Analysis of the Novels of Ruth Prawar Jhabvala and Kamala Markandaya,* National Book Organisation, New Delhi, 1988, p. 37.
22. Thumboo, *Journal of Indian Writing in English*, 8-12 (Jan-July) 1980, p. 112.
23. Kamala Markandaya, *A Silence of Desire*, Hind Pocket-Books, New Delhi, 1965, pp. 79-80.

    (All subsquent references are to this addition and the page numbers are given at the end of the quotations in parentheses.)
24. Ananda K. Coomaraswamy, "Young India", *The Dance of Shiva: Essays on Indian Art and Culture*, Sagar Publications, New Delhi, 1976, p. 158.
25. Uma Prameswaran, *op. cit.*, p. 103.
26. M.K. Bhatnagar (ed.), *op. cit.*, p. 103.

4

East-West Encounter

Possession

Possession is a very remarkable fictional work of Kamala Markandaya. In it, she highlights the inter-cultural conflict against the background of inter-personal and social situations which reflect the general inter-racial obstacle. The whole novel revolves round the cultural opposition of East and West. Here, the search of Valmiki for identity gets meaning against the background of the inter-cultural situation when he is suddenly shoved into a totally alien country, England, and a different set of values. Kipling's familiar line "East is East, West is West, and Never the twain shall meet!" is true. Markandaya pinpoints the cultural gap:

> Undiluted East had always been too much for the West; and soulful East always came lap-dog fashion to the West, mutely asking to be not too little and not too much, but just right.[1]

The novel begins with the meeting of Anusuya, an observer-narrator, with a beautiful, witty Lady Caroline Bell and the meeting presents the clash of personalities as well as of cultures. Anusuiya utters:

> She was supremely confident, born and brought up to be so, with as little thought of fallibility as a colonial in the first flush of empire, as a missionary in the full armour of his mission, dogged by none of the hesitancies that handicap lesser breeds. (p. 15)

Further, the relationship between Anusuya and Caroline develops on the lines of the England-India relationship. The two different cultures are represented here by them. Caroline comments:

> "Do you know?" She said "we go out of our way to meet, and we squabble every time we do. It's a sort of love-hate, relationship, don't you think? Like the kind Britain and India used to have!" (p. 70)

Valmiki, called as Val, the central figure of this novel, is forcibly adopted and 'possessed' by a rich assertive English widow, Caroline. His artistic genius is commercially exploited. The economic disparities of the East and the West underlie the patronage of Caroline of Valmiki's art. The sharp differentiation of culture is vividly presented through the situation of Val. In the beginning, Val is absolutely unable to think about himself. Hence, he willingly goes into the hands of Caroline. He wants to escape from his restricting native atmosphere and to lead a better life with the Englishman as he is not accepted in his society. He grew up with other 'rejects' of society like the mad woman and the crippled in the wilderness outside the village. He appears to be a passive peasant boy, who is very crude and unshaped. He does not want to accept the patterns of behaviour of the society he belongs to. He finds himself alienated. He is considered as an idiot in his community as he does not follow the routine affair of the society. He, the victim of social taboos, desires to elope with Caroline. He is fourteen years old and is regarded soft in his brain by his parents also, but he is an artist. Caroline takes fancy to the boy and thinks that his talents will be wasted in the wilderness, poverty and starvation. Five thousand rupees as a 'compensation' to the boy's parents is given by Caroline. She says:

> He must come away with us now at once. He's wasted here. (p. 10)

Caroline possesses him and deprives him of his power of thinking about himself. She renounces her responsibility for a spirit of possession. When she decides to take him away, she is suggested by Surya:

> It'll be entirely your responsibility. (p. 11)

Val is presented here at this stage very innocent and simple. When he gets the information that he is going to be sponsored by Caroline, he becomes extremely happy:

> He went over to Caroline, who had been watching us intently all this time, took her hand and gently, briefly laid his cheek against it the way a dog will sometimes thrust its muzzle into your palm. (p. 12)

But before leaving the village Val seeks permission from the Swamy, his mentor. Caroline tries to prevent him from going to the Swamy and the devas, but the boy prevails. Caroline with Val first takes shelter in London at a dull locality as Val is not polished enough to mix with the people of her class. Proper education and training mould the lifestyle of Val. He is able to communicate in English, a language which was foreign to him initially. But the assimilation of the foreign culture was not always a dismal result for it could "rise beyond grotesquerie to become unique and splendid, like the British in India, like Caroline overcoming the worst of foreign temperament and terrain" (pp. 85-86). Gradually, the boy grows physically strong and attractive:

> Two years had gone by, the skeleton had put on flesh, the human being stood taller, straighter, broader, with ruddy health instead of touched with the yellow of creeping enervation.... Whatever else might be in balance, this much Caroline, had done for him.[2]

Val is now able to fulfil the nymphean needs of Caroline, though she is twice his age. But before he is caught in the maelstrom of sexual relationship with Caroline, he gets Ellie, Caroline's maid, with child. She is a crippled girl of twenty and is one of the victims of inhuman cruelty perpetrated by the Nazi army. She lost her identity. Val and Ellie both had the same social origin. She had a very painful past. During the war, she had been kept in concentration camps and had been raped many times over. The painful and miserable life of Ellie attracts Val and he draws many images of this girl and tries to bring out the hidden pain in her being. The association of Ellie with Val becomes a constant worry for Caroline, Val's complete devotion to Ellie gradually arouses Caroline's supine sense of jealousy. His love for Ellie is not based on 'art for art's sake'. It is a bond of human attachment bred of passion, mutual understanding and sympathy for each other. With the heart of true artist, he is very loyal and faithful to Ellie. But Val is liked by Caroline also and she wanted him at any cost and hence, one day Ellie disappears mysteriously.

Val, an innocent rustic fellow, gets complete transformation from his visit to England. He becomes sophisticated and begins to indulge in it as a mode of escape from his ownself. He becomes an artist of a fashionable world. He is launched by Caroline into the fashionable world by making him the centre of attraction at a glittering party:

> The glitter-dust seemed to fall agreeably on Valmiki. Assiduously attended by slim young woman in black, he was floating around the room like an exotic sunflower, smiling, flushed with the champagne continuously at his lips.... (p. 109)

He is taken to a continental tour by the smart and resolute lady Caroline to exhibit his art and to earn name and fame. She tells about her plan to Anasuya:

> He ought to exhibit abroad to get really known France, America, perhaps Italy—besides there is all the experience, he won't get it all just from London. (p. 68)

In fact, the escape of Val into sophisticated London circle makes him more and more restless. An alien culture with different value system puts him into atrouble. He has lost his identity. Caroline is even jealous of the Swamy. The Swamy is the benefactor and patron of the art of Val. It is natural for the disciple to be attracted towards his Guru; so with the arrival of the Swamy in London Val is with him. As Val believes:

> He was like father and mother and friend. (p. 55)

The Swamy, a holy man, is like a father, mother and friend for Val. His visit to England, at the invitation of his English disciples, revitalize the cords of culture. Caroline is deprived of the love of Val during the visit of the Swamy to London. She has no courage to face the Swamy. She knows that Swamy's love for Val is a kind of spell which all the sages by nature are capable of exerting even if it is spiritual. In spite of the disparity in the age and race of Caroline and Val, there is a craving for possession in the heart of Caroline. Val is a highly sentimental young man who comes to know that Caroline has used all tricks to eliminate Ellie from his life. She used to send false letters in the name of Swamiji. Hence, he wants to keep himself free from the control of Caroline. He very woefully narrates his miseries to Anusuya:

> She has played with me—used me—treated me like a fool. (p. 151)

Caroline loses him again in the hands of another charming, young woman called, Annabel. She is only eighteen years old, small and slim with a soft mouth. Youth has its own charm and appeal; therefore, he is attracted towards Annabel. Caroline is much older than him, while Annabel is nearly of his age. The relationship of Val and Annabel goes smoothly for a brief period. Caroline starts playing mischief with Val again. In a party organised by Caroline she refers to Val's painting of Ellie. Annabel has no knowledge of Ellie before; Caroline's reminding the painting of Ellie remarks:

> Quite an obsession of yours, wasn't she Val's darling? It was nothing but Ellie for a long time. (p. 205)

Now the table has been turned by Caroline. Annabel accuses him of being ungrateful to a woman whom he loved in the past:

> You got her into trouble and you got out quick and curled up those holy eastern sentiments of yours about the sanctity of life. (p. 207)

Failing to understand the evil intention of Caroline, Annabel deserts Val in an utter disgusting position. The sense of possession of Caroline does not allow her bed-partner to lie with another woman. She desires to keep him under possession so that she can dominate over him:

> Except that Caroline was not only possessed, but had also taken in possession. (p. 183)

The exploitation of the have-nots at the hands of haves is presented here. The exploitation of the artistic consciousness of Val is very similar to Henry in Jame's Roderick Hudson. Raizada opines:

> It may be described as an allegory of the direction the independent India has to follow in its onward march to its progress. It poses a question as to whether India has to cut itself off from its roots and shape itself in the image of materialistic West or seek its growth from the life-giving springs of its own culture.[3]

Caroline means nothing in the original life of Val. She cannot pull herself away completely from her social superiority and continues making fun of the Indian sense of punctuality. He realises it after getting inspiration from the Swamy. S.N.K. Rao says:

> Ultimately Val realises that wealth cannot bring inner peace and that Val's story shows the belief that creative talent is to be used for the divine if one is to achieve inner tranquillity.[4]

The Eastern concept—'art is divine,' is here perceptible. When Val comes back to India he stays with the Swamy. He is followed by Caroline after three months. Being impatient, he decides to meet the Swamy. She argues that the Swamy would not continue to stay with him as:

> He has tasted other satisfactions that I have given and which he knows I can give...one day he will want to be mine again. I shall take care to make him want me again: and on that day I shall come back to claim him. (p. 232)

Caroline fails to understand Val's sentiments, the sentiments of a born Indian artist. The Swamy and Caroline represent two divergent approaches to life, the spiritual, i.e. Oriental and the material, i.e. Western. Uma Parameswaran remarks:

> Lady Caroline Bell is an autocrat, typical of the British Raj in India. She sets about getting possession of Val with the same dedication and ruthlessness with which the British subjugated India. She moulds him into a man, an artist and a lover after the image which she has in mind, and in the process, ruins him, depleting him of independence and spiritual strength, tough in her opinion he gains more than he loses.[5]

Val remains a true artist with a free and open heart, which cannot easily be subdued by a foreign agent, though a woman. Margaret P. Joseph rightly observes:

> While she succeeds in the first three—making Val a well-known artist, becoming his mistress, teaching him her materialistic values—she fails in the last, for in every crisis he turns to his mentor the Swamy.[6]

Caroline having bought Valmiki in body cannot possess him in soul. Val could not shake off his belief that "a part of God dwelt in everyman and would one day reunite with the divine whole" (p. 154). The possessiveness of Caroline is similar to that of the British for colonial India. Val himself says:

> She does not care for me. She cares only for what I can do, and if I do it well it is like one more diamond she can put on the necklace

> round her throat for her friends to admire; but when I do nothing I am nothing to her, no more than a small insect in a small crack in the ground. (p. 55)

He remains complete vegetarian in alienation also. He says: "killing has no appeal for me" (p. 178). British contact had blunted his prejudices but not his belief in them. He utters: "Animals aren't created for me! He considers the death of his pet monkey Minou as punishment for the violation of this precept (p. 178). Furthermore, the monkey symbol images the British with a cannabalist characteristic.

The theme of East-West tension is kept constantly in this novel. The word 'possess' has repeatedly been used here in there. Even the verbs used express this desire to hold, keep, exploit, claim, crave, dominate, mould and care. The metaphors have little to identify than as being particular to the Indian scene. Val improves his English gradually. He first speaks to Anasuya in Tamil. At first he learns to say 'no' in English. His vocabulary too is extremely limited. But later on he became able to speak good English fluently. Markandaya, therefore, becomes notable in adopting the tonal rhythm, vocabulary and expressions of the English language spoken differently by the speaker of English from different parts of the world.

In a nutshell, the present novel brings to light the sharp contrasts of the culture of East and West. Margaret Joseph says:

> Caroline is obviously England queening it over her. Colonies, possessor of India, its benefactor and despoiler is one. Val is India, illiterate but spiritually whole and gradually influenced for the worse by Western society.[7]

Further, H.M. Williams opines that *Possession* "is one of the most forceful artistic explorations of the distortions of India's national character in the British embrace and of her consequent urge to be free."[8]

Thus, the East-West cultural encounter is very sharp here and the novel is an excellent commentary on the Indo-British relationship. Mr. Rao has rightly said:

> In *Possession* the village artist and the Western blue stocking come together in a bizarre relationship which throws into relief not only the tensions inherent in a collision between two cultures but also the tragic-comic fluctuations of the individual sensibility which are recorded, by the narrator as Jamesian 'Central-consciousness'.[9]

The Coffer Dams

The Coffer Dams is another mature work of Kamal Markandaya. The conflict in the fiction lies in a real encounter between Indian and English engineers. The theme of the novel is based on a number of burning issues like, as Madhvi Menon and A.V. Krishna Rao opine:

> Tradition and modernity, freedom and responsibility, business attitudes and human values, a rational approach to Nature and an instinctual perception of vagaries and moods of the nature, and, above all, on that hackneyed and totally irrelevant issue, that is the juxtaposition and interaction of Eastern and Western attitudes.[10]

The present novel revolves round the construction of coffer dams by an English engineering firm called Clinton, Mackendrick and Co. The dam is constructed under the supervision of the Chief Engineers—H. Clinton and Mac Kendrick. According to the agreement with the Indian Government, a number of Indian engineers and other subordinate staff are engaged. But the Indian engineering personnel have to play a subsidiary role. Further, the Indians and the Europeans live in separate colonies, in virtual segregation, with their separate clubs, canteens, etc.

The novel under discussion highlights the hatred of the British and even Indian officers towards the hill tribesmen of

India. The dam is being built for the betterment of these tribals. But very unfortunately, they are humiliated and extremely exploited by their own employer, Clinton, who is the Western pragmatist having no humanistic concerns in professional task. The character of Helen is quite different from him. She is enlightened with healthy outlook. She does not believe in castes, creed and colour, but is the true worshipper of humanity.

The novel presents the value of human sensibility and relationships in the face of technological progress. In the construction of dam, Howard Clinton is sincere and prompt to finish it successfully. He continues his work despite severe pressures and unavoidable circumstances. It is going on even at the cost of humanitarian values. He has a very strong determination to complete the task and hence, he does not want any kind of obstruction in it. He says to his wife:

> My work, he said, from mounting conviction, which loomed tall as a mountain now; my dam, my business.[11]

The East-West interaction is not only on the level of people but also on that of ideas. The author portays the sharp cultural clash in terms of the humanistic concerns and technological progress. We are reminded here of Thomas Hardy's anxiety for human values. The Europeans, the new colonists, have a very different attitude to India.

> From within the invisible stockade thus thrown up, the new colonist peered at the vast sprawling enigma that they felt India to be. Some like Clinton, with a total lack of interest; some, like Helen Clinton, with a great, consuming curiosity and effortless identification; some uneasily, reluctant to advance into territory whose strange codes and values made them as unsure of themselves as pigeons roosting on anti-pigeon jelly; but most of them with rising tides of superiority lined and laced and made heady by fear, a nameless unvoiced fear, that to step outside was a

> hazard whose culmination would be a total, terrifying absorption of identity in an unknown ocean. (p. 32)

The rise of a dam means also the imposition of new values—commercialism, material comfort and alienation from tradition as noticed in *Shadow from Ladakh* (1966) of B. Bhattacharya. The novel also highlights that the choices of the individual in a changing milieu are determined by technology. In the beginning of the novel, Clinton and his wife Helen are leading a happy married life, though she is never allowed to interfere in his professional business and he himself does not peep into the privacy of Helen. His main motive is that she would completely indentify herself with his responsibility—to complete the dam.

Helen goes forward from his marital responsibility in search of an illusory freedom. She is in dire need of freedom as she is burdened with the constraints of marital life with Clinton. She gradually becomes aware that fulfillment lies in building up bridges of understanding. She gets lesson from the sustaining tribal tradition. She observes beyond the British perception of the natives as were "black apes"; she sees them as alive, sensitive men and women, and not "blank opacities of total incomprehension" (p. 29). She has a desire to rebel against conformity to the standards of the group. She regards that any cruelty to fellow humans is unforgiveable. The tribals are forced to vacate the place just for making bungalows by the British engineers. The tribals are regarded as 'animals' by Clinton and some other Englishmen. Helen declares:

> Don't human beings matter anything to you? Do they have to be a special kind of flesh before they do? (p. 107)

Helen's crave for freedom is also reflected in her affair with Bashiam. Bashiam is the educated tribal who, though his roots are attenuated, finds satisfaction in the richness of team spirit and professional achievement. Helen is attracted by his sense of responsibility and devotion: Her sense of freedom is similar to Simrit of *The Day in Shadow* of Sahgal and Rashmi in *This Time of Morning*, Parvati of *This Alone is True* of

Sarabhai and Sita in Padmini Sengupta's *Red Hibiscus*. Her rebellion against group conformity is a positive search for meaning but freedom from the constraints of social structure is negative one and according to Markandaya it is not fruitful.

The relationship of Helen-Clinton is successful even after a drift as it is based on mutual respect and understanding. Clinton himself realises his guilt about Bashiam's accident and this bridges the gap between the couple. Clinton earnestly says:

> "I did not wish to destroy", and Helen responds with: "If you are sure; and he accepts her."[12]

The meaning and impact of growth of the individual in relation to an alien culture is expanded by the experience of Millie Rawlings also. She also notices the strange spell of the country; she tries to forget it at parties and in her consciousness on which impinge the noise, the dust and the stress of living in this mysterious cultural milieu. Markandaya is not against material progress but affirms that, in the process of change, human values should not be lost.

The conflict in *The Coffer Dams* is accentuated in real encounters between the Indian and the English engineers. The English engineers visit India with memories of the colonial past. Jackson comments:

> It was indeed like a home from home. (p. 5)

They go ahead to build their little England in the orderly scene:

> The trim square plots of emerging gardens, the gravelled paths, the white washed boulders that demarcated and upheld private property rights. (p. 5)

Precautions are taken against the dangers of drinking polluted water and living in 'tiger country'. Simply they believe that no good would come out of the association with the Indians and the Indians want to keep away from the English because of their new found independence and also because they are convinced of their culture being superior to the others. The English who feel pride being well advanced in technical knowledge are doubtful if the Indians would ever be able to get 'in the bone' of the Englishman. They are full of superiority complex. They act as a real sahibs and 'mems' shopping in a big city. The project, a symbolic link between the East and the West, is not accomplished easily:

> So that Mackendrik felt that for two pins he would have risen and spelt out DAM, in letters of some white fire that would burn painfully, and perhaps purify, leaving only what mattered. (p. 187)

The modern industrial progress causes a great loss to the traditional value. The self-sufficient farmers and villagers are suddenly deprived of their means of income and their contented peaceful lifestyles; they are compelled to move to factories and industrial areas. They are forced to adopt the unstable commercial values instead of traditional cultural moral values. The present fiction is very close to Hardy's *Tess of the d'Urbervilles* as the root is the same.

> Clinton has no trust in the Indians as he considers them to be "a people who worshipped birds and beasts and probably snakes, decking the forest with scruffy hutches which they knocked up out of driftwood and crammed with leaves and flowers for their deities" (p. 76).

But his wife Helen reminds him of their own beliefs like: "One does not walk over graves wearing jackboots" (p. 186). Both Mackendrick and Helen think that Clinton lacks inhumanity. Mackendrick notices, "he seems to miss out somewhere on the human level" (p. 63). Helen comments on him for being inhuman.

In the Indo-British encounter, Clinton plays the role of ruthless imperialist imposition of his will on a colony. The natural resources are exploited by him. Without thinking about the ancient ethics the physical and cultural landscape are changed.

In the civilization-aboriginal encounter, the dichotomics is vivid—the dam could be the central image and metaphor. Like the imperialists desire to civilize a colony, modern civilization imposes its will and builds a dam that will ruin the aboriginal's way of life. But in the nature-industrialization encounter, the imperialist city culture invades nature and sacrifices those who live in step with nature in order to conquer and subjugate nature.

Clinton and Mackendrick at first establish their control over the tribals by flooding them out, and then train them to serve the masters like Macaulay's plan to educate Indians during British rule. Hence, the old traditional culture of the colony has been wiped out very strongly and the tribals are forced to depend on them for their living:

> The Company of Mackendrik that paid by far
> the healthiest wages in the area. (p. 69)

But Mackendrick towards the end of the fiction becomes sensitive to the needs of the Indians and has softer business ethics than Clinton. At the final phase, Clinton also admits silently his guilt about Bashiam's accident. Mackendrick tries his best to convince him to understand the risks the tribals would face. Mackendrick says, 'The people', thus expressing the value of social responsibility. But the opposition he faces from his wife and his partner opens his eyes.

The central conflict of the novel is between primitivism and modernity, the primitive man and the machine. Indians represent primitivism, while the British stand as the messengers of modernity. The river has a symbolic meaning in the sense that it embodies the life and religion of the Indians. It is a source of their food and livelihood. It is worshipped like Goddess. It is related to their life as it provides relief when the monsoon fails. At the same time when the river is flooded, their crops may be inundated and their huts are in a danger of being swept away. Hence, it is 'demon' to the Indians and a 'bastard' to the Britishers. This 'demon' is a devil to Britishers. Thus, the fiction presents the sharp conflict between the river and the dam, between nature and machine or as a clash between primitivism and modernity.

In the accident that took place, forty workers have lost their lives, two of them jammed between boulders. The workers, led by Krishnan, demand that bodies be relieved, defying Clinton who had decided on incorporating bodies and boulder into the last span of the Coffer dam rather than spending time blasting under water so as to release the bodies. In an earlier accident, two British workers were killed and their bodies had been rescued at the risk of sinking the boat. An equal treatment is demanded by Krishnan for the Indians who are dead. But Clinton firmly rejects the demand as unreasonable:

> "I do not understand", such preoccupation over something which is lifeless and irrelevant, when there is so much at stakes. (p. 190)

Thus, Clinton is projected as an unfailing monster who uncaringly sacrifices human beings and human relationships. Mackendrick on the other hand, plays the role of an ideal man, a counterbalance to Clinton; he combines in himself the positive qualities. His perception is very deep, so far as understanding of the complexities of Indians is concerned. Clinton embodies the forces of ambition and his wife, Helen, personifies the forces of humanitarianism. Helen says about Indians:

> I just think of them as human beings. (p. 6)

According to A.V. Krishna Rao and Madhavi Memon,

> Helen emerges as one of the connecting figures, bridging the gap between East and West and more specifically, between human values and industrial progress.[13]

Mackendrick understands better than the other Englishmen the problem of Krishnan, the leader of the Indian delegation, regarding the time-schedule of the construction of the dam:

> Mackendrick glanced at the Indian with something like sympathy. (p. 12)

But the inhuman attitude of Clinton forced Krishnan to think:

> Brush us off like flies, he thought, hurt and insult like splinters under his skin; despise us because they are experts and we are just beginning. (p. 13)

Above all, the relationship between Gopal Rao and Lefevre is very friendly:

> His growing friendship with Gopal Rao, over the last few months, had opened vistas which he found fresher, and distinctly more appealing than the limited view which fright and older counsel had ushered him into taking. (p. 61)

Lefevre bestows a nickname, 'Gecko' or lizard, to Gopal Rao. But being a Brahmin, it does not suit him and Lefevre understands it:

> But Gopal was a Brahmin, to whom the consumption of flesh, blood and carcasses was a necrophiliac activity unfitting for human beings, and he did not care to be associated with geckos, whose transparent stomachs grew black with the insects they bolted. Lefevre took his point and gracefully gave way. Their association bounded happily along on his give-and-take basis. (p. 62)

Consequently, the present novel deals with the themes of East-West confrontation in the light of tradition and spirituality versus modernity and technology. Prema Nanda Kumar declares:

> The theme of Kamala Markandaya's *The Coffer Dams* is material versus spiritual values, as the theme of Tagore's *Mukta-dhara* and Bhabani Bhattacharya's *Shadow from Laddakh*. The novel is well constructed and the end satisfying. The hysteria that can be generated by the political time serves against idealistic enterprenuers resulting in the victimisation of innocent aboriginals is well brought out. The novel seeks to lay bare the

> human problems so conveniently forgetten by the plain protagonist in favour of heavy engineering industries.[14]

In short, *The Coffer Dams* undoubtedly works on the periphery of East-West theme.

The Nowhere Man

The confrontation of the East-West is echoed once again in the novel, *The Nowhere Man*. Markandaya pays her sincere attention towards the real social interaction under the surface of inter-cultural tensions. It is a deep study of the helplessness of Indian expatriate who suffer all the life due to dislocation in Britain. The utter loneliness of the protagonist, Srinivas, in England makes him alienated and isolated. Assisi, C. Francis remarks:

> In *The Nowhere Man* Markandaya is more concerned with unfolding the sense of alienation of Srinivas, or the modern man. In this novel political considerations occupy a secondary place, the primary purpose being to highlight the isolation of the individual soul and expose the pathos of the human condition. Markandaya succeeds in achieving the delicate balance between unfolding the individual's psychological, and social predicaments and portraying a wider cultural and political setting which create these crises.[15]

Young and energetic Srinivas with his teenaged wife Vasantha visited England when India was still under British rule. Regarding the title and theme of the novel, V. Rangan comments:

> *The Nowhere Man*, as the title indicates, is a novel about a displaced Indian (South Indian Brahmin to be precise), Srinivas who settles down in England, but unfortunately not fully accepted by the English community. Srinivas becomes a rootless, restless, individual dispossessed of India and disowned by

> England. Though the predominant theme of the novel is displacement, alienation, and a search for identity in alien environs, it treats of larger human relations rendering the work and interesting psychological study of human relationship as well as of the essential human loneliness.[16]

Hari Mohan Prasad believes:

> *Possession, The Coffer Dams and The Nowhere Man* are fuller explications of the East-West encounter; they are even more than that, a sensible vindication of India's spiritual heritage and deep humanity.[17]

Not similar to her earlier fiction, which is set in India, this novel is situated in England and provides opportunity to notice the clash of cultures from a different angle. Markandaya suggests that the adjustment and acceptance of a country has to be on both sides otherwise, there is rejection and the consequent footlessness. The thrust of the novel is rightly reported in the studies like Between Two Cultures:

> All groups who come to settle in a strange country have difficulties adjusting to new way of life. Asians in Britain feel particularly acute problems. Strongly attached to their own religions, languages and customs, they feel that the Western culture is a threat to their values and traditions, and so they tend to become isolated. Hostility and racial discrimination from the host community further prompt Asians to seek support from their own groups. As they strive to preserve their culture and identity, it becomes harder for them to 'assimilate'—to be accepted as British.[18]

Srinivas, 'the nowhere man', was born in a South Indian Brahmin family. The family later shifted to the city where Srinivas's grandfather built a large house. This family was related to another family here. Srinivas's father, Narayan, after completing his higher education, became a lecturer in a government college in the city. Being a brilliant student, Srivinas entered the college where his father was employed after passing the school examination. He stood 1st in the University Intermediate Examination. The college had a British Principal and Deputy Principal. Many of the teachers were also Englishmen. Srinivas's father, being an Indian, was superseded by the English teachers in promotions. He was forced to live at the mercy of the British Government. His silent spirit of resentment is not lost on Srinivas. The involvement of Vasu's family in the national struggle makes Srinivas feel ashamed of the fact that his family has kept itself not only aloof from it, but his father has continued in government job. He returns his gold medal for his success at the intermediate examination to the Principal. His father though timid, too makes a symbolic gesture. He discards his English suits and goes to the college in Khadi dress. Srinivas finds himself "festooned and foundering in question marks...."[19]

Narayan, a staunch loyalist, also rebels against imperialism by singing an Indian hymn at the college function. He was humiliated and stopped by the then Governor, the chief guest. But Srinivas comes to the defence of his father and tells the Governor to take his bloody hands off his father. He is blacklisted. He plunges into anti-government activity such as the manufacture of petrol-bombs in collaboration with Vasudev, Vasantha's brother.

He is now in an awkward dilemma:

> He would have fled from himself too, but he did not know how. (p. 130)

He is in dire need of peace:

> All I want is peace, said Srinivas, starting at himself, stranger in the glass; all I want is peace. Is that too much to ask? It seemed so. (p. 131)

Narayan is confined for a time in a mental ward, while he has been branded as a terrorist. Hence, he has lost his chance to lead a normal life in India. His career is bleak. Consequently, he is driven to England with his newly-wedded wife, Vasantha, and sets up spice shop in London.

Srinivas becomes the baffled expatriate who attempts to reconcile East-West values in the alien society in which he decides to take shelter to escape from a worse situation in India. Vasantha is the embodiment of Indian culture. She deviates from English ways and English habits as she feels herself firmly rooted in her own culture. She does not allow herself to accept, in any way nor does she let Srinivas do that. She persuades him to purchase the house at No. 5, to establish their identity. They seldom mix with the English people. The theme of alienation begins with their complete detachment from the English society and the association culminating into a condition of mind. The situation of Srinivas is very close to Dev of Anita Desai's *Bye, Bye, Blackbird,* and Timeri Murari's Leela of *The Marriage.* The feelings of alienation become intense in Srinivas. The cause of this alienation is the cultural shock. His alienation is due to his migration to England and not by choice but by force and he never feels at home in the alien surroundings; further, he is an idealist and a self-effacing man whose values hold no importance at a time when the overall atmosphere is of one of uncertainties during the war years. The cultural displacement has insulated Srinivas and his wife from the British community. The natives also have hostile stance to the immigrants:

> These immigrants they keep coming here, who asked them. One day they are poor, living off the rates, the next day they buy us all. (p. 197)

They are hated very firmly by the young generation. They want them to be ousted from the country. They are not going to accept them:

> "Immigrants," said Mike, "Filthy mob bringing filthy habits with them". Ought to learn them a lesson or two, said "Hygene and that." Ought to be kicked out, said Fred, who invited them here. (p. 222)

Without doubt, Srinivas becomes a victim of racism. He becomes a soft target of Fred Fletcher, a neighbor but a misguided young man, who tortures him badly in many ways—places a dead mouse on his doorstep, abusing and slandering him and finally burning him alive by setting fire to the house. Srinivas's demise is an ugly end of individual fanaticism:

> BLACKS GO HOME, they said, their fear and hate crystallised into words which opened whole new hells of corresponding fear and desolation in those at whom they were aimed. (p. 168)

The image of the dead mouse is significant and the differences of attitudes of Srinivas and Mrs. Pickering show the general cultural differences:

> "Well" she said shortly, from being served, "it was only a mouse." (p. 225)

The alien is always the alien. Vasantha has brought with herself a sandalwood box filled with Indian soil and the bottle of the Ganga water preserved by her, having both symbolic and realistic significance. It shows here rootedness:

> Vasanta in her breath or bones had remained wholly Indian. She would have liked her remains committed to the currents of an Indian river. (p. 39)

Simply, Vasantha's sandalwood box and the bottle containing the Ganga water which are disposed of with her ashes into the Thames do not merely move one, but they also become a cultural metaphor.

Vasantha leaves this unreal world because of tuberculosis and Laxman does not come even to attend his mother's funeral. Now the alienation of Srinivas is extreme:

> That period, for Srinivas, was a dust bowl of being. Empty. Without meaning. Scooped out, picked clean, no climbing up the slippery sides. A skull from which all matter had gone. (p. 40)

After the death of Vasantha, he comes across Mrs. Pickering, a divorced and as lonely as he himself. She teaches him to accept the English culture and finds himself one with it:

> If one is cut off from one's culture, there is always the adopted one to draw upon. (p. 68)

The best of India and England meet in the relationship between Mrs. Pickering and Srinivas. Uma Prameswaran is right to observe that the relation between the two is the relationship "between the best of India and the best of Britain".[20] She has opened his mind to the country which in a way Vasantha has cooled off. She helps him in his financial crisis; she even cares for him till the last. After his death when Dr. Radcliff mourns and thinks that the English community was the main cause of his death, "and we have all had a hand in it" (p. 298). Mrs. Pickering rejects it saying:

> "Why should I"? I cared for him! And indeed, that seemed to her to be the core of it. (p. 299)

Srinivas is absolutely unable to resolve the problem of his identity. He is the nowhere man. His leprosy becomes the outer manifestation of his isolation. It is also a sign of the repellent nature of racial hatred. Fred said, "you will never make me a leper" or "I will never let you forget you are a leper" (p. 269). Leprosy limits Srinivas's freedom. The disease is a symbol of his alienation. He himself feels isolated:

> I am a stranger, he said. I have been transformed into a stranger, said the unwanted man and examined a pair of hands whose stigmata would be the excuse. (p. 230)

Even after fifty years he realises that he is an Indian:

> Their world. Mrs. Pickering's world which struck most strangely of all. To which she, and they, but not he, belonged. Inhabited an area devoid of meaning for him, but dense with experience for them. It isolated him, cast him in the role of intruder. (p. 173)

The cultural ties of the East cannot be abolished by the expatriate Srinivas and his wife Vasantha. She is shocked when she receives a telegram from her son about his marriage to an English girl, Pat:

> The way these Indians went to pieces. Different from one's own kind who would close the door and pull down the blind decently, not stand about letting the whole world see. (pp. 31-32)

They feel that their son has left them to live alone:

> Srinivas did not argue with his son. He has moved far away from us, he told himself.... They parted...when I am better, she said to her husband, we must return to our country. There is no reason, now that India is free, why we should not. She said painfully "Is there anything, really, to keep us here anymore." (p. 36)

The clash between the immigrants and their children is very sharply described in the study of *Between Two Cultures*:

> The parents cannot understand why their children wish to give up the culture they have held for centuries, and the children cannot understand why their parents are old fashioned, illiterate embarrassing.[21]

Further, Rekha Jha opines:

> The younger generation in England wish to stem the inflow of coloured immigrants.[22]

Srinivas and Vasantha are typical Indian immigrants, carrying Indian habits, dress and beliefs to an alien land and leading a peaceful life but without, in any way, assimilating the culture of their adopted country. Vasantha always wears a sari, a nine-yard sari. Normally, most of the immigrants women would like to wear Western clothes. Srinivas wears "tight white trousers and a black coat" (p. 4). He, further, takes off his shoes before he enters his apartment. He and Vasantha both remain vegetarians though their sons are non-vegetarians. Usha Bande points out:

Through Srinivas, Kamala Markandaya portrays the character of a man who is an amalgam of both the Indian and the Western values and who is unable to solve the conflict produced by the two contradictory systems. On the one hand, he is an Indian in his disregard for materialism:

> He does not want to possess property in England lest he be tied down to the soil; on the other hand, he follows a bohemian way of life and accepts the Western mode.[23]

In short, we can say that in *Nowhere Man* Markandaya has presented the vision of East-West encounter in the specific milieu of Indo-British relationship. Thakur Guruprasad says, *The Nowhere Man* is

> a remarkable work of fiction depicting the tragedy of bicultural living in all its horrowing aspects.[24]

Indeed, the novel holds forth the possibility of an inter-cultural meeting point. The clash of cultures is also very vivid in Santha Rama Rau's *Remember the House,* B. Rajan's *The Dark Dancer,* Nayantara Sahgal's *A Time to be Happy* and Raja Rao's *The Serpent and the Rope.*

Thus, *Possession, The Coffer Dams* and *The Nowhere Man* portray the East-West encounter in the best and the most effective manner. They exhibit an element of positive closeness, not that of negation or opposition, between the two cultural strands. Sincere efforts for the union and reconciliation are explored here. Obviously, Markandaya's "good man and woman come from both cultures."[25] Markandaya delineates graphically tensions and conflicts between two different races from various perspectives by bringing them together.

NOTES

1. Kamala Markandaya, *Possession,* Jaico Publishing House, Bombay, 1994, p. 110.

   (All subsequent references are to this addition and the page numbers are given at the end of the quotations in parentheses.)
2. Quoted in C.V. Venugopal, "*Possession:* A Consideration," *Perspectives on Kamala Markandaya,* ed. Madhusudan Prasad, Vimal Prakashan, Gaziabad, 1984, p. 151.

3. Harish Raizada, *Indian English Novelists: Some Points of View,* K.K. Publications, Delhi, 1996, p. 114.
4. K.S. Narayan Rao, "Religious Elements in Kamala Markandaya's Novels", *Ariel: A Review of International English Literature,* 8-1 (Jan. 1977), p. 45.
5. Uma Parameshwaran, *Texas Quarterly,* 11, 2, Summer 1968, p. 239.
6. Margaret P. Joseph, *Kamala Markandaya,* Arnold Heinemann, New Delhi, 1980, p. 49.
7. Margaret P. Joseph, *op. cit.*, p. 50.
8. Quoted in Venugopal, *op. cit.*, p. 151.
9. A.V. Krishna Rao, *The Indo-Anglian Novel and the Changing Tradition,* Rao and Raghavan, Mysore, 1972, p. 138.
10. Madhavi K. Menon and A.V. Krishna Rao, "*The Coffer Dams*: A Critical Study", *Perspectives on Kamala Markandaya,* ed. Madhusudan Prasad, Vimal Prakashan, Gaziabad, 1984, pp. 163-64.
11. Kamala Markandaya, *The Coffer Dams,* Penguin Books India Pvt. Ltd., New Delhi, 2008, p. 127.

    (All subsquent references are to this addition and the page numbers are given at the end of the quotations in parentheses.)
12. Quoted in A.V. Krishna Rao and Madhvi Menon, *Kamala Markandaya: A Critical Study of Her Novels, 1954-1982,* B.R. Publishing Corporation, New Delhi, 1997, p. 97.
13. Krishna Rao, *op. cit.*, p. 102.
14. Prama Nanda Kumar, *Indian Writing in English, Three Cheers, Indian Literature*, Volume XIII, No. 4, 1970, pp. 36-37.
15. Francis C. Assisi, "Homage to Kamala Markandaya." Online:http://www.beilharz.com/authores/markandaya/p.3, Accessed on 3/31/2007.
16. Madhusudan Prasad, *op. cit.*, p. 186.
17. Hari Mohan Prasad, "The Quintessence of Kamala Markandaya's Art," *Response: Recent Revelations of Indian Fiction in English*, Prakash Book Depot, Bareilly, 1983, p. 164.

18. Foreward to *Between Two Cultures:* A Study of Relationships Between Generations in the Asian Community in Britain, Commission for Racial Equality, London, 1978.

19. Kamala Markandaya, *The Nowhere Man,* Orient Longman, Bombay, 1975, p. 113.

(All subsequent references are to this addition and the page numbers are given at the end of the quotations in parentheses.)

20. Uma Prameswaran, *A Study of Representative Indo-English Novelist,* Vikas Publishing House Pvt. Ltd., New Delhi, 1976, p. 90.

21. *Between Two Cultures*, p. 7.

22. Rekha Jha, *The Novels of Kamala Markandaya and Ruth Jhabvala*, Prestige, New Delhi, 1990, p. 35.

23. Usha Bande, "Kamala Markandaya," *A Companion to Indian Fiction in English*, ed. Pier Paolo Piciucco. Atlantic Publishers and Distributors, New Delhi, 2004, p. 103.

24. Thakur Guruprasad, "And Never the Twain shall Meet: Kamala Markandaya *The Nowhere Man*", Language Forum, Special Issue on Modern Indo-English Fiction, 7, 1-4, April 1981-March 1982, p. 199.

25. C.D. Narasimhaia, "Other Indian Literatures English," *Comparative Indian Literature*, Vol. 2 ed. K.M. George, Madras, Macmillan, 1985, p. 1302.

5

Problem of Identity

A Handful of Rice

Alienation constitutes the most striking theme in Kamala Markandaya's fifth novel—*A Handful of Rice*. The novel 'fictionalises the sociology of India'[1] by awakening the polite society to the plight of the rural people. The protagonist of the novel, Ravi, feels a strong sense of alienation throughout the novel. He is a vagabond and as a proletarian product of the fifties, he is enmeshed in the maelstrom of change, in the transition from traditional and rural society to the machine-ridden, materialistic urban milieu. Usha Bande holds the opinion:

> Kamala Markandaya shifts her attention, in *A Handful of Rice* (1966), to the exodus to the cities by the rural poor and the socio-cultural economic problems the uncertainties of urban life. It is the story of a peasant boy who comes to the city, undergoes a crisis of character, as he is lost in its labyrinthine mode of life, but is saved from further degradation by his basic value system.[2]

A Handful of Rice deals with hunger and poverty and the consequent degeneration of human values like those in *So Many Hungers* of Bhabani Bhattacharya. It presents the melancholy, maladjustment, emotional imbalance and psychological instability of a modern man. Ravi gropes for a world where he can breathe freely, a society where he can eke out a living independently. He struggles for a place in the society, but socio-economic pressure pushes him back to his assorted destiny. Ravi, an educated son of a peasant, would like to have a "decent way of life in the city where he is outsider without caste, in a no-man's land between coolie and clerk".[3] He is forced out by "the relentless pressures of their existence, in the upsurge of revolt that had begun to dismantle the old pattern of family life first in one village then in another."[4] Ravi is everyman and represents the predicament of modern man. The novel centres round Ravi's struggle with hunger as the novel is about urban life with its struggle for survival.[5] Furthermore, Eliot's view "those who sit in a sty of cotentment meaning death"[6] is true to the life of Ravi. He can be compared with Eugene O'Neill's the Hairy Ape, who is neither a beast, nor even a full man.

Ravi, like numerous innocent village youths, has drifted to the city with the golden dreams that he would thereby escape hunger and death and live an honourable and peaceful life. In the city, he goes to the memory lane and looks back to the village from where he has come and remembers the people who lived there:

> All lived between bouts of genteel and acute poverty—the kind in which the weakest went to the wall, the old ones and the babies dying of tuberculosis, dysentery, the 'falling fever', 'recurrent fever', and any other names for what was basically, simply, nothing but starvation. (p. 12)

Obviously, it is not true that the city has to provide better prospects to the poor to lead a happy and better life. In the city, there is absolutely nothing as such. The novelist observes:

> The city had nothing either, although they did not discover this until they arrived: but it held out before them like an in can-descent carrot that one day, some day, there would be something. (pp. 25-26)

To get rid of impoverished conditions, Ravi takes refuge in the city but the city disowns him. He is dispelled and discarded. He is in the quest of identity. His neck is gripped by his poor financial condition. In the stifling and suffocating urban life of Madras, Ravi has the lassitude of hunger, and "the terror of losing his identity in an indifferent city, which was akin to death" (p. 27). He is always worried about his identity whether in village or in city. In the sprawling city people are insecure and there is violence, despair and disillusionment. S.P. Swain remarks:

> They hardly have any sense of social conscience and human values, where man ceases to have faith even in his own self. In such circumstances man becomes self-alienated.[7]

Life in a city like Madras presents the impression of a jungle. The author uses the symbol of jungle several times in the novel to indicate the kind and quality of life the urban Indian offers. When Ravi is staggering under the heavy blows of poverty, he finds himself in this jungle. Kamala Markandaya writes:

> He was alone in the jungle, and in the jungle one fought or died. The knowledge was an incandescent light at the core of his being like the single eye set in the forehead of a demon. Lying, sleeping, waking, even in his frenzied acts of love its beam scorched and excoriated him. (p. 217)

Ravi desires to lead a truly human life, however it is very hard for him:

> The humanscape in a city like Madras or, for that matter, in any other city in India, produces a decayed and decaying human life.[8]

Ravi barters his conscience and trysts with a band of diehard criminals and in course of time turns to be a member of the underworld smugglers. He is wandering like a rudderless-ship which finally lands him into the underworld of petty criminals. He is arrested one day by the police in a drunken state, but fortunately escapes and takes shelter in a house. Apu's wife ties his hand and foot and keeps a watch on him. In the morning, he is beaten black and blue. She takes pity on him and offers him some food to eat out of womanly compassion. While taking the breakfast, Ravi thought:

> If I had a wife, he thought as he ate, she would cook for me, it would be like this every day... but what had he to offer to get himself a wife?—I'll buy her a little house, small but nice, he thought as he finished, and some nice new shiny aluminum cooking vessels...and with a job one can save, say a quarter of one's wage. (p. 11)

Ravi recovers himself and confesses his guilt. City life proves a hell to him as he soon goes astray. Hunger and destitude compel him to go into the world of unlawful activities. In the morning when he sees Apu's young bright-eyed daughter, Nalini, he instantly falls in love with her reminding us of Shakespearean love at first sight. He dreams about her and ardently craves to marry her. He is enchanted by her charm:

> Soft and flushed from her bath, dressed in a pink mull sari with her hair loose about her shoulders. It was like a curtain, her hair: a shining silk curtain that rippled and shimmered as the ivory comb worked down from root to top. He hardly dared to breathe, he was so taken by the beauty of it, her grace, the lovely movement of head and rounded arm that curved and lifted her uncovered breast. (p. 34)

He wants to win over Nalini at any cost:

> Ah, Nalini, he thought, Nalini. She was worth it, worth anything, even worth giving up the sweet life for. He put it all on her, forgetting the trinity of hunger, drink and misery that had been intermittent companion to his sweet life.... (p. 40)

On the advice of Damoder, who initiated him into the world of diabolic city life, he goes to Apu's house on the next day of incident and offers to put the bar in the window which he had broken the previous night. He does the work without any cost, though he is given money by Jayamma, yet he refuses it. He listened to his inner voice and decides to mend and resolve. Finally, he would like to bid goodbye to the criminal world. He accepts Apu's offer of a job and decides to lead a gentleman's life. He notices the social and economic disparities in city life and feels depressed. He is against the dealing of Apu with the rich. He very firmly refuses to play the role of fulfilling Apu's desire. He is always after human values. He is not willing to adopt the code of conduct and the mode of dealings of Apu. He is repulsed to see Apu's bribing the watchman at the gate of a rich memsahib so as to get an audience with his prospective moneyed client. Being very gentle and soft, he does not want to take everything. He resents when the shopkeeper of the ready-made garments sells the clothes at higher price than was paid to the poor tailor. Ravi undersells his labour to Eve, the fashionable shop, which buys the clothes he stitches and sells it at a very high rate. He is astonished to see:

> One of their coats. It did not look the same here: it had become vastly richer, more sumptuous, since leaving his hands—he had to look twice to make sure it was the same. But there was no doubt about it, he could even see one little diamond where the gualting live wavered. Pleasure filled him. He felt like grabbing the nearest passer-by and pointing it out with pride, until his eyes travelled down the straw hand—span waist where the price tab was Rs. 125/- Ravi was stunned. (pp. 68-69)

Gradually, he loses some of his valued clients and suffer losses. Obviously, city proves as a seat of black marketeers, hoarders, bootleggers and cheat. "Grab or go under" (p. 117) are the watchwords of city dwellers. P.S. Chauhan remarks:

> The city becomes the symbol of...violence and inhumanity.[9]

Under the shadow of unfair social exploitation Ravishankar alone runs the family and shares all responsibilities of several persons as they all live on him—Puttanna Tangani, his husband, Kumaran, Verma, along with his own family. Niroj Banerjee says:

> ...for persons like Ravi who run away from the countryside and its impoverished conditions to take shelter in the city where financial constraints grip them by the neck.[10]

Above all, after the death of Apu he carries the responsibility of his entire family. But unfortunately his business shows a decline as he is not trained enough. As a victim of circumstances, he acts recklessly, he is not only unfair to Nalini but is also extremely callous towards other members of the family. He beats her and hence she suffers a miscarriage also. In acute frustration, he rapes his mother-in-law. In an alienated association with Damodar, Ravi gets life in all its raw—hunger, penury and exploitation.

> The trouble—to him, Ravi, first as city innocent, now as husband and house holder—lay in the working out of that "if" Damodar would have had no doubt at all, he never had any. What might be would be if you were prepared to do this, and this, and this. (p. 70)

Damodar is successful in digging at Ravi's respectability:

> If you like decent money, you know where to come. Of course you'll have to get rid of your beggar mentality first, otherwise you will never want decent money, will you? (p. 73)

But at each step Ravi's "responsibilities began to press down on him unpleasantly, reminding him of the money locked up in all those bundles of work, that lay..." (p. 119).

Ravi does not hate Damodar as he has a different Sanskara. Markandaya describes:

> Ravi respected him (Damodar) for it. He himself, he knew, would have gone in for rich food, for silk shirts and enamel cuff links: Yet his upbringing had taught him to focus inward, upon the constant light within, to see the

> raging obscenities and miseries to their life as essentially external and ephemeral, and for all that he angrily repudiated this teaching, shreds of it obstinately clung.... (p. 113)

He loves values which he got in his village and whenever he recalls in Madras he feels weak and pathetic. In the words of the writer herself,

> It sickened him that life: the misery and squalor, the ailing babies who cried all night long, the way one was always poor and everyone knew was always poor too, a cup of coffee every morning, a shirt without holes, a shawl made of pure wool to keep out the cold of a monsoon dawn; and to know that one never would. (p. 49)

Ravi is always in favour of a meaningful life as there is an urge of life-force in him:

> ...that life could be sweet, that it was meant to be sweet, that if it was not it should be made so. (p. 49)

His agony of helplessness is very vivid when his son is ill and his wife asks him for medical treatment at the night time. He cries out:

> A doctor, what! Are we, memsahibs or something to send for a doctor for every ache and pain? Will you pay his bill? (p. 228)

But he got his conscience very soon and repents. He calls a doctor but it is too late. The boy passes away of meningitis. It is the most critical moment in his life:

> But Raju could not hear. He had withdrawn, his mind dispossessed, his body jerking in convulsion. Terror was beating at Ravi, paralyzing wings, but he fought it off and gathered his child to him and held him tightly, feeling the kicking muscles and nerves as if they were joined to his own tortured body, not putting him down until they ceased. (p. 230)

At the crucial juncture, he renounces the moral code which has brought him to utter destruction:

> No more blocks and restraints. No more loyalties and responsibilities, for he had none. Neither to the land nor to people nor to their society nor to society's betraying ramshackle codes. (p. 231)

He blames the society for this:

> I don't blame myself for not getting the doctor. I blame them. Them. Society. Guilty of casual murder. (p. 23)

City life means a grim struggle for existence and survival. Ravi encounters a total collapse of culture and civilization here. He cannot become a part of such a civilization. Srinivas Iyengar rightly states the plight of Ravi who "is caught between the pull of the old tradition that all but strangles him and the pull of a new immorality that attracts as well as frightens him."[11]

He wants to lead a happy conjugal family life with Nalini. He longs for mental peace and emotional stability but in vain S.P. Swain opines:

> Ravi's struggle for existence and his attempts at self-realisation, his rebellions and recalcitrant stance are all symbolic of a thousand thrusts made unsuccessfully by sensitive, souls on a system that neither yields her responds. People like, Apu, Damodar and Nalini can adjust themselves to this system or rather to this anti-system. But Ravi with his saeva indignation can hardly do so. He is a square peg in a round hole. He refuses to fit in.[12]

He is indeed a social victim:

> But what could he do within the narrow frame of respectability he had slung round his neck like a penance? (p. 70)

Ravi is hankering after a luxurious life. He desires to live like the rich and affluent. When he visits the well-furnished and highly decorated house of the memsahibs, he is distracted to find the silk hanging, tall windows, gleaming doors and shining furniture. His dream is to live like this "without worry, without wanting every need and craving satisfied" (p. 83). Hence, he is compelled to see his life as a challenge. He often cries out:

> I want more. I want more. I want a bed... double beds, divans. (p. 75)

He appears to be very sensitive to the class structure:

> The class structure of the rich and the poor has taken firm root and disparities widen with the poor being deprived of basic essentials of food and proper medical care and housing.[13]

Despite his bad habits, Ravi is still in his 'primal' state as far as his beliefs are concerned. His actions reflect his love and compassion. He throws the plantain leaf on which his *iddlies* were served, to the cows nosing in the gutters. Apu's wife Jayamna too "had been brought up to respect every living being as the fragmentation of an eternal God" (p. 29).

In an utter desperation once he joins a mob shouting "rice, rice today" (p. 233). The rice godown is looted. He also goes very close to the ricebags, but unable to get even a handful of rice. Still he is always optimistic that a day of prosperity would come.

In another scenario, he indulges himself in looting and destroying the site of the rich people. He takes a brick to hurl at the locality of the well-off but he controls himself.

> Ravi took aim, poising the jugged brick level at his shoulder. But suddenly he could not. The strength that had inflamed him, the strength of a suppressed, laminated anger, ebbed as quickly as it had arisen. His hand dropped. (p. 237)

He becomes able to overcome his sense. He says, "But tomorrow, yes tomorrow..." (p. 237). Shiv K. Kumar describes the precise nature of Ravi's plight:

> But in the midst of an orgy of mob-fury, Ravi is caught up in an existential moment of soul-searching.[14]

Now he has lost the key to the underworld forever and the gates of the human world have been opened wide to him. He looks forward to the human world of emotion and conscience.

In short, Ravi is not in favour of submission to ignominious way of life. This integrity and fidelity of his self ultimately bring about his alienation. In depicting alienation in the character of Ravi, Markandaya displays her universal sympathy for those who suffer. Undoubtedly, she does have an experience of the slimy poverty and the dry husks of depair of the society.

Two Virgins

Two Virgins is a blueprint of the journey from adolescence to womanhood of two sisters, Lalitha and Saroja. As K.S. Sarma puts it:

> *Two Virgins* is a story of adolescence and growth of maturity in an Indian village of two sisters, Lalitha and Saroja.[15]

In the words of Usha Bande:

> The conflict between the traditional and the modern outlook, the rural and the urban ethos, the depth of wisdom of the older generation as against the shallow vanity of the new, has been clearly brought out through Lalitha and Saroja.[16]

The two sisters do not like to adjust to the squalor and poverty of their village life and desire for freedom and prosperity. Though both are born and brought up in the same atmosphere, they develop differently. Saroja is docile, obedient and timid, while Lalitha is bold, outgoing and manipulative. She aspires for glamour and autonomy. She is in focus by the help of her physical beauty and feminine charm.

> Lalitha had status. She had no husband yet, but everyone could see when she did, she would have more than her fair proportion.[17]

For her life means glamour, money and status and flying high above the clouds, she gets an opportunity to fulfill her desires with the help of the film magnate Gupta, though the man is not reliable. She becomes a victim of her own vanity and ignorance. Asha Susan Jacob observes:

> But lured by the glamour of the film world she falls a victim to the film magnate Gupta who refuses to take the responsibility of her pregnancy.[18]

If Lalitha is a child of grace, Saroja is the child of the soil. Saroja adheres to the cultural values and is never tempted by the glamourous world. Lalitha has her education in an English school, Three Kings School. She has been fascinated by her Anglo-Indian lady teacher, Miss Mendoza. She takes Miss Mendoza as a symbol of her dreams. Lalitha loved what Saroja hated and Saroja loved what Lalitha was indifferent to, Lalitha loved to be in the company of Miss Mendoza, Mr. Gupta, and her English school girl friends, whereas Saroja loved to be friendly with Manikkam's wife, Chingleput, and rustic boys and girls.

The older generation is very critical of Miss Mendoza's school with its Western notions of Maypole dance, free mixing up of men and women and the individualistic approach to life. Aunt Alamelu coaxes her brother:

> Brother, she said, it is not for us, puny denizens of this immoral age, to question the wisdom of our ancient mentors [...]. You have given your children rights, Brothers, and they have come to roost. (pp. 177-78)

Lalitha surrenders herself to the outer world of romance, pleasure and the neo urban culture. She is highly enchanted by the lifestyle of Miss Mendoza. According to her opinion, "it is barbaric not having a fridge" (p. 26).

She calls 'city' a 'heaven', her 'spiritual country', 'spiritual home' (p. 128). And hence, she leaves for Bombay silently and comes to Mr. Gupta, a big film director for a breakthrough in films. She craves for a role in a film to achieve all her material pleasures. On the other hand, Saroja is carrying in her heart the traditional belief in morality and contentment of village life. The two sisters have no meeting point at all. Lalitha would like to revolt against the primitive ways, while Saroja is satisfied in her home adhering to age old ideals. Dr. Hari Mohan Prasad opines:

> The innocence of the village and the lures of the city, the irresistible filteration of modern ways into ancient faith and custom emerge as contrasting sets and the pairs coalesce.[19]

Simply, the encounter between the traditional and modern Westernised values comes to the forefront in the portrayal of the two 'virgins' of the novel. According to Shirwadkar Markandaya, "explores the problem of the growth of a girl's awareness the change in her as she gets caught up in the swirling events around her and returns to the family fold and code of conduct but with her childhood innocence forever gone."[20]

Lalitha finds her dreams coming true when she is offered a role in a documentary film based on the village life, produced and directed by Gupta who sponsors her on the recommendation of Miss Mendoza. She is extremely happy over her success.

> "I feel happy," she further says, "I feel like a dove on the wing, I could soar away, away like an eagle to the topmost peak of the sacred mountain." (p. 21)

Lalitha leaves for city without the consent of her parents. She becomes quite defiant and obstinate. After a few months she comes back home pregnant. Unwed motherhood is the worst form of degradation and is not accepted by the traditional Indian village society at any level. Lalitha undergoes abortion and when her parents feel that they should all return to the security of the village, Lalitha again disappears into the city. The city is like a jungle here as one sees it in *A Handful of Rice* also; it makes her feel alone and powerless. Contrary to Lalitha her sister, Saroja grows up with the naive belief:

> It is a pity, some people are pretty, some people are plain, said Lalitha examining herself languidly in her hand mirror, Saroja knew which she was, but she had become used to being plain. (p. 13)

Saroja and Lalitha grow up in the traditions of Hinduism and hence they respect all the living beings. They strongly believe that 'you couldn't destroy soul'. But the teacher of Lalitha informs her that "souls did not enter other bodies. They went straight up to heaven or down into hell or were cooped up in purgatory, which was in between place, for doing penance in..." (p. 37). Further, it is said to Lalitha that the animals had been created for man and that God had given man dominion over the beasts. But she is not convinced at all. The two sisters live with Appa, Amma and a widowed Aunt Alamelu who had no husband and consequently no status. To Appa the liberated Westerner, the joint family is an anachronism. Aunt Alamelu feels it is directed against her and utters:

> Just tell me to go and I will, I know I have outlived my usefulness.... I am only a widow, less than the dust so do not torment yourself about my fate. (p. 18)

Mr. Gupta is presented here as a shameless rascal who exploits innocent girls like Lalitha. When Appa and Amma approach him, he blames the innocent girl for inviting him for sex:

> What she was doing in his studio then flapping her lashes and issuing invitations to all and sundry. (p. 182)

The result of Western influence that has ruined the Indian traditional society has been highlighted here. The problem of identity and alienation is very open in the portrayal of the two sisters. Lalitha faces the possibility of an identity crisis when she gets an exposure to the Western mode of living, S.C. Harrex remarks that Markandaya's novels comprise "a wide ranging awareness of the determinants of and threats to identify."[21] In the opinion of A.V. Krishna Rao and Madhavi Menon,

> ...the sense of identity of her characters always comes to be tested against social values. The sense of identity operates within the social context where the clash of different value-systems and attitudes causes concern. In such a dilemma, conformity is the key to individual happiness.[22]

Saroja selected the same solution to the problem of identity. But on the other hand Lalitha goes back to the city, regarding its life as an ideal one. She is out off from her village and hence there is no communication with her family at the village at all. Her identity in the city is neither positive nor socially acceptable. But Saroja receives a positive identity in her community.

Furthermore, the two ends of the tradition-modernity axis is represented by Appa and Aunt. Appa does not approve of the tradition of India and curses the narrow mindedness of the Indian society. He is a progressive liberal having little concern for the traditional culture while his sister Aunt Alamelu is a firm believer in social culture and tradition. She has a strong belief in the traditional effectiveness to preserve one from harm. She tells Lalitha:

> It's you that's shamless, said Aunt Alamelu grimly, throwing yourself at him, you're so full of this film star nonsense you can't see you're only making yourself cheap to him even if he says you're wonderful. (p. 104)

Lalitha would like to be the part of the modern life having a license of obscenity. But Aunt comments it as a shame and says to Appa:

> Mayploles, she said, dancing around them and such Christian practices, is it a fitting pastime

> for our young Hindu maidens?...no, it is shame-shame, totally contrary to the code of our Hindu decorum which has safeguarded the virtue of our youth for a thousand years. If it's gone on that long it's moldy, it stinks, it's high time it's ended! Shouted Appa. (p. 176)

The ideological difference between Appa and Aunt is represented here very brilliantly. Appa is in favour of keeping pace with the growing infleunce of Western culture. His dealings with his wife and his daughters are liberal and generous. The huge gap in the society due to casteism is also highlighted here. The society is divided in the name of caste. The differences in caste kept Mr. Gupta, the film producer, and Lalitha, the aspiring actress on different scales:

> ...the truth was that although both were Hindus, which was the important thing, their levels were different.... Unequal society. (p. 179)

Further, Appa reminds Amma of Gandhi's preaching that all are the children of God but Amma rejects it. She believes that "it is their Karma, their fate" (p. 39) to have been born into that caste. Marriages are solemnised in India between the couple of the same caste. Even stars play an important role:

> ...the star you were born under had to be in harmony with your husband's. If it were inimical the marriage was doomed...you couldn't have been allowed to marry in the first place. (p. 205)

The Western outlook of Miss Mendoza and the film-maker Mr. Gupta, her high heeled shoes and his cream silk suits all these are denounced by Amma and Aunt. She was a Christian and in the view of the two Hindu ladies:

> Spitting and hawking were the uncleanly habits of the Christians who did not mind about spittle, thought nothing of using the same drinking cups. (p. 176)

Western society subordinated everything to the motive of bigger profits on the economic front. India had been reduced to beggary as English goods had been thrust on it, and as a result, its own handicrafts dwindled. Amma believes that English doctors with their advanced skill think themselves as superior and that the Indian doctors are influenced by them.

In a nutshell, the novel prefers a blending of two cultures to a dissociation of the Western one from the Indian one. What A.V. Krishna Rao and Madhavi Menon observe is remarkably noticeable:

> Two virgins exhibits thus the preoccupation of an Indian woman novelist with tradition and modernity, social evils and tensions, the crisis of character arising from the changing values of modern civilization in relation to traditional Indian society.[23]

Pleasure City

Rikki, the culturally alienated product of English education, is the mainstay of the Kamala Markandaya's last novel, *Pleasure City*. He emerges as an ideal individual out of an East-West encounter on the level of cross-cultural understanding. According to A.V. Krishna Rao and Madhavi Menon,

> The situation of the novel is almost the same as in *The Coffer Dams*: the instrusion of technology into a non-descript fishing village jeopardises the traditional occupations of the villagers and imposes on them alien set of values, attitudes and decisions. It upsets the traditional systems of thought and social behaviour and scales of values. Commercialism, individualism and materialism enter the original lifestyles of the simple fisherfolk. (Rao, p. 157)

Meeting-friendship-parting is the central theme of the novel. There is a fishermen's settlement near a sea-shore. There is a fisher boy, named Rikki, who is a pupil at Mrs. Bridi's charitable school which she runs for the benefit of poor orphans. Markandaya presents a graphic description of the poverty and hardships faced by the fishing community by the introduction of Rikki. He has lost all the members of his family at the sea but has learnt to accept the blows of fate stoically. Intelligent and artistically oriented, Rikki learns from Mr. and Mrs. Bridie various skills like making tiny models of cathedrals and ships, and also pebble mosaics. D. Maya observes:

> Rikki's imagination had been touched and toned by the British missionary couple, the Bridies who reluctantly chose to make India their home when the Empire fell. Through the English books, the Christian religion and the culture transmitted by them, the fisher boy developed dreams and aspirations unknown to a community waging its relentless battle with the elements. He even develops a nostalgic longing for England, cutting him off from the community.[24]

A multinational corporation named the Atlas International Development Corporation (AIDCORP) has accepted the assignment of building a holiday resort in the coastal village of Rikki. The corporation is founded by an Englishman named Boyle who is its chairman, but, as the author tells us "...half a dozen nationalities were represented on the Board, and could be cited or produced in each zone of activity: And, as many were dotted among the senior executive."[25]

Toby Tully, an Englishman, is one of the directors. He is the grandson of Sir Copeland, the resident at the princely state of Devapur in pre-independence India.

The sea-resort is developed into a city by AIDCORP and is popularly known as 'Shalimar'. It is the modern version of Emperor Shah Jahan's pleasure garden in Lahore (as also in Kashmir) from which it takes its name "the luxury pleasure complex which at blueprint stage, with rare unity, and not entirely cynically, got to be called Shalimar by everyone concerned" (p. 66). Besides a luxury hotel named Ashoka, a tourist complex, comprising sea-side villas, a lake called the Blue Lagoon, a wrestling arena, an airstrip, etc. are constructed by the AIDCORP.

The knowledge of English brings Rikki close to Tully, who becomes his patron, and he is appointed caretaker of the swimming pool. Tully notices the boy or youth.

> He had noticed him briefly the day before, for his fluent English—he had come bearing some message for contractor from the headman. (p. 39)

Tully and Rikki forge a friendship that sees them through the building of Shalimar and the renovation of Avalon. Rikki undergoes a complete transformation. He has been hypnotised by the glamorous world of the Shalimar and hence he dislikes the pitiable life of fisherman. He feels sick of the poor house of Apu and Amma which had given him shelter and had become his home when he had been left a shelterless, helpless orphan.

> He was...sick of the mongy hut, even the thatch was tattered. These days he scarcely regarded it as his home.... (p. 137)

As A.V.K. Rao and Madhvi Menon observe:

> Rikki and Tully unconsciously desire freedom from the division of race and class-consciousness. For them, ultimate freedom seems to lie in an escape from these kinds of constraints. They make the efforts to restore channels of communication that had been blocked by centuries of oppressive colonial rule.[26]

Further it is described:

> At first, Rikki is merely attracted to Tully but slowly he starts defying the conventional barriers of race in the atmosphere of Shalimar, where people have built narrow walls of racial divisions.[27]

A close tie is formed between Rikki and Tully despite a wide gap between their social status. Notwithstanding the difference, the two learn to appreciate and accept each other. They like and need each other. They enjoyed together:

> And Tully, aiming for a late soil, would come upon him in the evening, after pool duty, standing in the prow, singing. Not film hits, which he favoured, but one of those ditties, haunting, slightly tiny, that, early on one, heard the women singing when the fishing boats rode on. (p. 328)

Tully establishes contact with Rikki on a level of equality and gathers knowledge from him of the sea and the fishing-folk. He comes to place more faith in Rikki's instinctive knowledge of the land and the elements than in science or reason. Tully gets communion with Rikki because he transcends the corrupting influence of race, nation and culture and attains "a quality of simply being that washed over them like water or light and merged them into the one landscape" (p. 147).

Rikki, the fisher boy, at first works as a waiter in one of the posh restaurants at Shalimar and later serves as a life-saver for the swimmers at Shalimar. Valli, his adopted sister, starts working as a sales girl in a dress shop. Yet the love for sea of Rikki does not fade away, as it is his part and parcel. He has to choose either his fishing or working in a Shalimar. He is in catch 22 situation. Hence, economic conditions are such that it is really a Hobson's choice for Rikki when it comes to the question of survival. He is forced to accept the situation by the circumstances. Thus, Rikki transforms himself from native fisher boy to a polished human being. Ambuj Kr. Sharma says:

> Markandaya has successfully presented almost all the important aspects of life. She has presented a large variety of her themes with a rare realistic touch. She doesn't idealise or glorify but points a realistic picture of Life.[28]

Rikki the dreamer is found dreaming of Akbar's city:

> Rikki had forgotten its name and there was no one to remind him. But a similar city was rising, his imagination supplied in extraordinary detail. (p. 28)

But Rikki is able to observe the spoils prowling round the new city that is arising:

> Far away place-names stencilled on the crates, trutle from the Andamans, teas from Assam and Sri Lanka, quail, lamb, pink grilled salmon ledden in ice, and lush scarlet berries on refits on straw-rare and sumptuous fare garnered from around the land, fit to grace an emperor's table. (p. 65)

Rikki, like Valmiki of *Possession*, is also a character that is leaving his boyhood behind. Val gets transformation from a herdboy to an artist of international fame. Rikki's artistic skill progresses and flourishes when he comes into the contact with Tully.

Rikki desires to be economically independent in the environment of Shalimar. Tully would like to go into an ideal realm where language does not matter. Their friendship is based on understanding. Rikki tells Valli: "He is as human", he said, "as a you or me" (p. 73). And Tully accepts "Why under the skin he's not that different" (p. 81).

The choice of a lucrative job by Rikki is sharply contrasted with Mathur's love of tradition and custom who likes to continue fishing. Rikki, like Ravi and Rukmani, is a victim of economic change. The reaction of Appu is the representation of the villager's unwillingness to accept modernisation. Still, he is a helpless victim:

> The old man was brought in to consult. He was the headman, to whom should they refer if not him? but Apu's headmanship was based upon a different kind of living. He did not have answers to their questions. (p. 26)

Further, Apu says in vain:

> This is our territory. The waters are ours, to a five fathom depth. (p. 26)

In the characterisation of Rikki the sea imerges as a powerful image. It is the sea that brings him close to Tully. It is also the sea that divides the East and the West, and further

Rikki from Tully. Tully himself accepts that there is an ocean between them. Rikki goes to the sea and gives "himself up to sumptuous solitudes of ocean and seashore" (p. 292).

Again, Tully also reflects "a mineral sea" which is still until "ruptured by sudden emotion" (p. 326) which could be his feeling for Rikki. The contrast between technology and tradition is based on the construction of Shalimar and the reconstruction of Avalon, a dream-mansion of Arthur Copeland. AIDCORP has men who noticed that the future lay in "fulfilling widespread and mistful longing for progress: progress out of a wretchedly unacceptable poverty and backwardness into something that decency could stomach" (p. 21). It "never allowed private feelings to interface with and admirably distilled purity, of purely technological mercenaries" (p. 21). In the background of the reconstruction of Avalon, Tully and Rikki meet on a personal level. Thus, Avalon emerges out as a symbol of an understanding of the East and, at the same time, of an ideal realm of peace. Shalimar is the only resort for Rikki to earn more money; it is an escape from economic disability. Avalon is typically British, whereas Shalimar is Indian. Avalon shows the growth of intercultural understanding also. If Shalimar is the product of technology and progress, Avalon is the path to human concern. The quality of Avalon is symbolic too:

> Avalon: as Heblekar walked, reflective, up the finely cambered path. Avalon, with its towers and dreamy terraces and the vigilant common, as had been envisioned by the man who built it, and captured in its flawed magnificance by that unknown artist's hand. Impermanence, it went without saying, in all structures: an imperative, and vital, absolescence woven in. (p. 272)

Avalon provides an opportunity to bridge the gap between one perception and another. In the words of A.V. Krishna Rao and Madhavi Menon,

> In spite of the colonial connections, the ruling race had handed down the racial arrogance and

> prejudice it had nurtured, and that is why even in the atmosphere of Shalimar, it is difficult for the general run of Westerners to look upon the local fisher folk even as human beings.[29]

The present novel highlights the optimistic attitude that the new can learn from the old to forgive and forget and live together. In the larger interests of humanity, unnecessary pain and anguish can be overcome. Rikki, while trying to save Corinna, gets injured his leg and is hospitalized. Corinna is quite different from Caroline of *Possession*:

> She too felt that something was being broken down, and said quite simply as she was now able, I'm sorry, Tobby. About Rikki, I mean, it was unforgiveable. I must have been mad. (p. 317)

Mr. Tully, her husband, would like to console her:

> Rikki's ending. He asked me to tell you. All in one piece, he thinks. (p. 318)

Furthermore, before leaving she has to do many things; first is to make peace with Rikki. Then:

> She did, with an unassumed humility and courage. As for him, he found he could not continue to hate her, now that she was leaving. (p. 319)

When both the husband and wife, Mr. and Mrs. Tully, rushed to the airport, they talk about the boy:

> "Thank heaven he's mending". "Yes I'd never have forgiven myself if keep me posted, will you, darling?" "Of course". (p. 319)

The feelings of Zavera for the boy is also remarkable. She picks out a sweater. Knitted in striking, even lurid, wool, she feels the vivid garment would please that poor fellow in hospital. Again:

> She had gone to visit, taking a jar of sweet meat and the brilliant pulover to cheer up the

> poor boy, and expecting only thanks, also received this surprise. (p. 321)

Mrs. Adeline Lovat also goes to see Rikki:

> Perched an envelope, with her cheque, coyly concealed inside, on the locker beside him, you'll soon be better. (p. 333)

The departure of Tully from Shalimar is unbearable for Rikki:

> ...he had always accepted there were limits to Avalon. Except that Tully had invaded too strongly to be silenced now, the permeated fabric returned him, the halls and corridors were echoing, the mansion throbbed with his presence. (p. 341)

The memory of the friendship in Rikki's consciousness is vividly concretised:

> Rikki wandered in and out of the rooms, looking listening, not really surprised by what he heard. Tully had given Avalon life; it belonged to him. The throbbing was a measure of what it was giving back, a natural return. (p. 341)

He starts working on the incomplete mosaic which has been laid for Tully. He leaves it only after he has finished with it, and goes down the hill from Avalon:

> His cheeks were still wet, he realised, as he walked. He wiped them dry, wondering as he did so why he bothered. It was quite dark by now, there was no one around to see. (p. 341)

Uma Parameshwaran opines:

> But perhaps he is worse off than Val at the end of the novel, because Val had matured as an artist before he was thrown to the wolves but Rikki is left alone on the threshold of manhood while Tully returns to England.[30]

A.V. Krishna Rao has rightly observed that the novel stresses the fact that:

> The time is ripe for a proper permanent friendship between the east and the west but it depends on the effort of the human race to make allowance for one another.[31]

Usha Bande remarks:

> A mutual understanding and respect for each other's point of view replaces the East-West conflict.[32]

In short, Markandaya has tried to reconcile East with West in the *Pleasure City.* She has attempted her best to convey that there are no boundaries between East and West. The blending of the two cultures which stand poles apart from each other is implicitily pin-pointed here. The harmonious relationship between Rikki and Tully is a brilliant example of cultural assimilation. It shows the fact that the people of different nations can still love each other in spite of cultural differences. There is a sacred bond of humanity which binds all the people together and makes them realise that all the world is a big family and all human beings are the part of a simple family in spite of the huge gap between different nations. *Pleasure City* is a sincere attempt to harmonise relations between the East and the West. The people of the East are slowly adjusting themselves in the modern complex setup of the West.

The Golden Honeycomb

The problem of identity is once again witnessed in Kamala Markandaya's magnum opus, *The Golden Honeycomb.* This most ambitiously designed novel holds a significant place because it focuses on the Indian history during the British rule and presents the fate of the native princes affected by the historical events. It is a chronological account of the Devapur state and the helplessness of the rulers rendered by the cunning Britishers. The novel further depicts very vividly the relations between the English and the Indian princely states on the one hand, and the native princes and their subjects, on the other, though tenuous and tension ridden. A.V. Krishna Rao and Madhavi Menon observe:

> The novel images the interaction of three groups of society in the late 19th and early 20th centuries—namely, the British rulers, the Indian princely clan and the Indian common man.[33]

The novel is a window to the East-West encounter. Usha Bande remarks:

> The English wanted to hold on to the country that they called "a gem in the British crown" and as the prologue to the novel records, they adopted all means fair or foul to tighten the noose around the native kingdoms. Consequently, the rulers of the states all over India remained weak and almost the mouth-pieces of the British regime whereby they alienated their own subjects.[34]

The three generations of the Indian history, as represented by the three Maharajas of Devapur State—Bawajiraj I, II and III respectively, are handled in this novel. Bawajiraj I is deposed for his nationalist inclination and a Kshatriya young man is selected to ascend the throne as Bawajiraj II. He is chosen to act as a puppet king to safeguard the interests of the English masters and he proves himself the same. After the death of Bawajiraj II in a hunting expedition, his young son is made Bawajiraj III under the Dowager Maharani's supervision. He has been brought up and educated strictly in accordance with the norms of the British Government. He is very loyal to his British masters and always ready to safeguard their interests and respect their sentiments. His English tutor provided him an unsolicited testimonial:

> I have seen his highness grow...into a tall young man whose distinguished appearance can be said to match his inner quality. A fine horseman, and excellent shot, a first class cricketer and unrivalled at Polo, his highness is equally the most charming of hosts.[35]

Kamala Markandaya makes a shrewd comment regarding his education that it was calculated to make an English country gentleman out of the scion of Indian rulers that Britain desired. He is a great admirer of the British. But his mother, Manjula, has some instinct of oneness with the people from whom her son has been alienated by his education. He has a concubine named Mohini and he falls in love with her. He is a slave to her beauty and physical charm and has a son by her, named Rabindranath, after the renowned poet and nationalist. Rabi is born in 1895 and is the central figure of this novel. Bawajiraj would like to marry Mohini also, although he is married to a princess named Shanta Devi so that Rabi may accede to the throne after him, since he has only daughter by Shanta Devi. But Mohini does not want to marry him and she refuses to become a Maharani. She wants freedom from the curbs and adverse forces, hence she rejects it:

> "I don't want to be your queen, I want to be free". "Am I not free?" "of course you're not free". "As far as I'm aware". "You're aware of nothing. The British have tied you up hand and foot and you don't even know it. Do you want me to be shackled like you? (p. 32)

Further, she says:

> I can make you happy without that. I have no wish to be your second wife either. (p. 32)

She maintains her freedom and makes the king accept of the doctrine of equality. She wants to inculcate nationalist feelings in Rabi and hence a Pandit is engaged. Indian culture, history and literature are taught to Rabi. He hears the tales of the former glories of the ancient and war-like race by his mother and grandmother. His feelings regarding the people are different from his father's. The tension is balanced very skilfully by the author. Bawajiraj is partly Westernised and pro-British and is played upon by the Dewan and the Agent, Sir Arther Copeland, whereas Rabi, his son, is more democratic and is more influenced by the nationalistic feelings. He comes closer to Janaki, the sweeper girl and Das, the gardener's son. He further meets Sir Arther and his children.

Then he meets the daughters of the Dewan, delicate Brahmin girls brought up in an extremely orthodox manner. He realises the utter servility of his father at Delhi Durbar. He is particularly irked by this abject reality:

> Leaning forward, gripping his seat with excitement, Rabi watches his father, sees him pause and speak and bow, three low bows. Watches him retire. Sees the shining warrior-king retreat, walking backwards. Backing away like a lackey, like one of his own subjects at one of his own durbars. (p. 116)

Later, Rabi wishes that Bawaji could be got rid of:

> So that he could reach the periphery of an understanding of himself. (p. 227)

He starts brooding over:

> The reverberation came all right, but oddly muffled by what had been amassed by secret unremitting processes at conscious and unconscious levels; those doubts, inflections, obliquities, what speech expressed and slurred over. (p. 237)

Rabi realises that India has sold her freedom to the British. But he is suddenly confronted with the sense of a responsibility that cannot be shirked. It seems to him as if the "muted years had suddenly begun to bell and toll in his ears." (p. 240). If Janaki is the first agent of Rabi's growth, Jaya is the second. His sexual relationship with Jaya is an escape into negative freedom. Paul Roubiczek remarks:

> We shall remain free only if we choose actions which give substance to freedom and increase it; if we merely act as we like, we may succumb to unnoticed compulsions from within or without and thus bury our freedom again.[36]

Rabi notices that the true freedom does not consist in satisfying his physical needs. Strikes have been started by the exploited, oppressed workers of the textile mill in Bombay:

> The mill workers who, among other things, disputed the Maharaja's programme (of taking delivery of a fleet of imported Rolls Royce luxury cars at the Bombay port dock) by striking did so because they were driven. What drove them was desperation, although sinister labels were found for their driving force. Nothing sort of desperation, at this stage in their history, would have stirred them to challenge the established order. (p. 250)

Watching the mill-workers' strike Rabi says:

> "It's one's duty", he says and people's livelihood is our responsibility. (p. 276)

Furthermore, the Bombay scenes highlight the problem of identity also. At the outset he seeks his identity in the case of Jaya but in vain. Again, after the strike, the workers go back to the mill because they are conscious of their responsibilities towards their families and would "off-load guilt on to the innocent shoulders of wives and children" (p. 288).

Rabi finds that things appear in a new light. His spirit begins to rebel against the curbs invested in the person of a Maharaj Kumar, he has to select between contrary value-systems. Thus, he is in mental conflict and the threat of identity is very vivid here. Iredale declares that Ravi symbolises, "the emergent people of the state, the consciously classless new men and women of India."[37] Rabi's actions appear "both incomprehensible and profoundly irresponsible" (p. 415) to Bawajiraj. He develops honest differences of opinion with his beloved father. Later consideration and understanding become an important factor in Rabi's personality. The East-West theme is handled very brilliantly here by the author in presenting the relationship of Rabi with Sophie, the white-skinned girl. In the final Holi scene Sophie shows her intimacy but Rabi retracts as he remembers that there really is a barrier between them, the barrier of culture which cannot be crossed. Rabi further tells Sophie:

> People aren't different, in the things that matter. (p. 455)

The confrontation of East and West is also depicted very sharply in the novels of B. Rajan and Bhattacharya. The Whites and the Blacks are divided by political and cultural barriers here, like Mahmooda and Saleem of *The Walls of Glass* who are divided by the India-Pakistan barrier. Iredale aptly remarks:

> ...the book is a study of manipulation and conflict, and as in *Two Virgins* (1973) the central issue is the growth of the child through gainful experience to an understanding of the complex adult world which he must enter and in which he must struggle.[38]

Rabi wants to lead a complete life. He shares his desire with Sophie:

> I want the moon. A full round moon, nothing less will do. (p. 429)

We are reminded here of the desire of the child Rama of the Ramayana. He is in favour of freedom and he later joins the crowd that only asks for freedom—an individual's birth right. The problems of social, cultural and economic adjustments between the East and the West are keenly observed in this novel. Mutual love and understanding can only remove the difference of water-tight compartments. The Englishmen of India believed themselves superior and wanted to keep distance from the Indians as the Indian culture was scorned and considered as barbaric. The Indians themselves were divided according to caste. It was based on their birth and it could never be acquired. Each caste was designated with its own work. The Brahmins held the highest position. They were regarded as the men of learning and therefore, they were priests and Prime Ministers like the Dewan in this novel. The Kshatriyas had second order in that social category. Being of the warrior class, they were the rulers but even the ruler had to bend to touch the Brahmins' feet. So this social structure was interwoven. At the time of the appointment of a new ruler of Devapur, the British despite their power were not able to overlook the caste order. At first one of the Vaishya caste was selected but this was a caste of traders and the English, ironically traders themselves, were not allowed to tamper with the accepted social pattern.

The man-made barriers are depicted very nicely here. The Brahmin Dewan and the English Resident were both professionally similar, learned in their ways, punctilious in their dress, fastidious in cleanliness yet there was a distrust among them. Having a strict code of purity and cleanliness the Brahmin changed his cloths and bathed "after the hurly burly of audience to rid himself of the scent of natives and 'feringhi'" (p. 6).

Every person other than a Brahmin is considered as polluted and the foreigners are extremely polluted as they are not vegetarians. A distance is made between the Brahmin and the British Agent. The Brahmin Minister did not enter the birth chamber at the birth of the prince because it was 'unclean' and would do so only after purification. The Dewan's wife Vatsala did not want the Resident to defile her household by crossing its threshold. When the Resident did so, he had to walk in his stockinged feet. After he had drunk from a silver goblet, Vatsala had it melted down to purify it.

The dewans and Panditji are conscious of their own intellectual superiority and have a kind of arrogance. They themselves are intensely conscious; they are brahmins and so expect much of themselves:

> ...it is not a dignified performance, nor one even remotely within the scope of himself the twice born Brahmin. (p. 23)

Furthermore, the relationship between Rabi and Sophie's the revelation of something common between the two cultures. Sophie is praise of Indian cultural life is a continuation of the East-West encounter. Sophie and Rabi go on excursions, adventures and outings; they have cast away whatever strangeness existed between them; they were enjoying birth days and festivals without any reservations. Both of them gave instances of friendship and intimacy:

> She was in love with India, sharing his (Rabi) passion for country without the tap roof of

> birth that was his, that sturdily provided support and sustenance during the worst seasons of doubt, dislike, confrontation and even at times hatred.[39]

Thus, love for their country and interest in its happiness embodied in the trinity of equality, liberty and fraternity were the bonds of their friendship.

The cultural life has been presented by Mary and Arthur, Bawajiraj III and Shanta Devi, Tirumul Rao and Vatsala and Bawajiraj III and Mohini. Mary and Arthur are foreigners and hence they behave and act in an English way. They feel free at home but out of home they preserve dignity and superiority:

> It is sanctuary within that magnificent edifice whose cadences in Sir Arthur's hearing are sweetened and magnified by the presence of his wife and the two infants.[40]

Bawajiraj has never loved his wife, Shanta Devi. Consequently, she is always gloomy and morose. She is no better than a royal doll. Bawajiraj and Mohini are not married —Mohini is a concubine and her son, Rabi, is the product of Bawajiraj's sexual diversions. But this illegitimate alliance has received the blessings of Manjula, Bawajiraj's mother. It is very significant to notice that Shanta Devi and Mohini both are indifferent to the affairs of the state, though Mohini is secretly interested in the cause of the people. In a nutshell, the cultural life with a sense of the blending of the two cultures is very vivid here. The novel is considered as Markandaya's "memorable faith accompli."[41] Here the author evokes through imagery how an Indian would not be entirely an Englishman by undergoing the British trading and by adopting the British manners and thinking. Bawajiraj III has assimilated the English quality of cruelty to the animals, but not their ethos. He symbolizes his degradation. It is clear when sympathy is evoked in the readers for the dying pig:

> Liver, spleen bladder all are ruptured, all kinds of mysterious fluids are spurting.... Before it gives up its piggy ghost it turns one furious eye upon the hunter while the second revolves with

it, a blind but glaring red-jelly of an eye. (p. 235)

An Indian appears to be an alien in his own land and a stranger in the country of his adoption. In short, Bawajiraj is alienated from his motherland by the British. The image of alienation of Aziz and Das in *A Passage to India* separating them by caste hatred is evoked here as well. Tirumal Rao like Prof. Godbole "goes to great lengths to keep a distance of six places between his persona and that of the Englishman" (p. 51). Therefore, alienation and Death constitute an important theme of this novel.

NOTES

1. K. Venkata Reddy, "A Tryst with Conscience: *A Handful of Rice*", *Perspectives on Kamala Markandaya*, ed. Madhusudan Prasad, Vimal Prakashan, Ghaziabad, 1984, p. 154.
2. Usha Bande, "Kamala Markandaya", *A Companion to Indian Fiction in English*, ed. Pier Paolo Piciucco, Atlantic Publishers and Distributors, New Delhi, 2004, p. 99.
3. S.C. Harrex, "A Sense of Identity: The Novel of Kamal Markandaya", *Journal of Commonwealth Literature*, Vol. VI, No. 1, 1971, p. 74.
4. Kamala Markandaya: *A Handful of Rice,* Orient Paperbacks, New Delhi, 1985, p. 57.

   (All subsequent references are to this edition and the page numbers are given at the end of the quotations in parentheses.)
5. K.V. Reddy, *op. cit.*, p. 155.
6. T.S. Eliot, *Marina*, L-10.
7. S.P. Swain, "Crisis of Conscience: A Study of Kamala Markandaya's *A Handful of Rice*", *Kamala Markandaya: A Critical Spectrum,* ed. M.K. Bhatnagar, Atlantic Publication, New Delhi, 2002, p. 79.
8. S.K. Nagendra, *Society & Self in the Novels of R.P. Jhabvala and Kamala Markandaya*, Sarup & Sons, New Delhi, 2005, p. 142.
9. P.S. Chauhan, "Kamala Markandaya: Sense and Sensibility", *Literary Criterion,* 12, 2-3, 1976, p. 145.

10. Niroj Banerjee, *Kamala Markandaya: A Critical Study*, Kitab Mahal, Allahabad, 1990, p. 93.

11. K.R.S. Iyengar, *Indian Writing in English*, Sterling, New Delhi, 1985 p. 446.

12. S.P. Swain, *op. cit.*, p. 82.

13. Rekha Jha, *The Novels of Kamala Markandaya and Ruth P. Jhabvala: A Study in East-West Encounter*, Prestige, New Delhi, 1990, p. 31.

14. Shiv. K. Kumar, *Osmania Journal of English Studies*, 7, No. 1, 1969, pp. 8-9.

15. Krishna S. Sharma, "Two Recent Novels of Kamala Markandaya", *Triveni*, October-December, 1976, Vol. XLV, pp. 28-35.

16. Usha Bande, *op. cit.*, p. 104.

17. Kamala Markandaya, *Two Virgins*, Vikas Publication, New Delhi, 1977, p. 13.

    (All subsequent references are to this edition and the page numbers are given at the end of the quotations in parentheses.)

18. M.K. Bhatnagar (ed), *op. cit.*, pp. 139-40.

19. Hari Mohan Prasad (ed), "*The Quintessence of Kamala Markandaya's Art*", *Response: Recent Revelations of Indian Fiction in English*, Prakash Book Depot, Bareilly, 1983, p. 163.

20. Quoted in *Kamala Markandaya: A Critical Study of Her Novels*, A.V. Krishna Rao and Madhavi Menon, B.K. Publications, New Delhi. 1997, p. 130.

21. S.C. Harrex, *The Fire and the Offering: The English Language Novel of India 1935-1970*, Vol. I, Writers' Workshop, Calcutta, 1977, p. 259.

22. A.V. Krishna Rao, *op. cit.*, p. 133.

23. A.V.K. Rao, *op. cit*, p. 139.

24. M.K. Bhatnagar (ed), *op. cit.*, p. 111.

25. Kamala Markandaya, *Pleasure City*, Chatto and Windus, London, 1982, p. 33.

    (All subsequent references are to this edition and the page numbers are given at the end of the quotations in parentheses.)

26. A.V. Krishna Rao, *op. cit.*, p. 158.
27. *Ibid.*, p. 159.
28. M.K. Bhatnagar (ed), *op. cit.*, p. 193.
29. A.V. Krishna Rao, *op. cit.*, p. 163
30. Uma Prameshwaran, *Kamala Markandaya: Writer of the Indian Diaspora,* Rawat Publication, New Delhi, 2000, p. 245.
31. M.K. Bhatnagar, *op. cit.*, p. 117.
32. Usha Bande, *op. cit.*, p. 108.
33. A.V. Krishna Rao, *op. cit.*, p. 141.
34. Usha Bande, *op. cit.*, p. 106.
35. Kamala Markandaya, *The Golden Honeycomb.* Chatto and Windus, London, 1977, p. 36.

    (All subsequent references are to this edition and the page numbers are given at the end of the quotations in parentheses.)
36. Raul Roudiczek, *Existentialism: For and Against,* Cambridge University Press, London, 1964, p. 122.
37. Roger Iredale, "Society and Self Knowledge in the Novels of Kamala Markandaya," *Tenor*, No. 2, Jan. 1979, p. 57.
38. *Ibid.*, p. 57.
39. Quoted in Neeraj Garg, *Kamala Markandaya's Vision of Life*, Sarup and Sons, New Delhi, 2003, p. 143.
40. *Ibid.*
41. A.N. Dwivedi, *Indian Writing in English*, Amar Prakashan, New Delhi, 1991, p. 39.

6

Conclusion

Receptivity is a characteristic trait of a perfect culture—a culture that allows the acceptance of other outsider influences while preserving its own native features. The East and the West, representing tradition and modernity respectively, have thier fine co-existence in the Indo-Anglian fiction. It has its very powerful reflection in the novels of Kamala Markandaya. Though not being a moral preacher, her message is oblique and implicit. She expects from her characters to think, feel, and act as common beings, since there is no greater virtue than the love for humanity. This is portrayed on the personal, social, political, religious and cultural levels. The issues related to the East-West dichotomy have been stipulated and reflected in her novels. As such her fiction is simply a product of the cultural ethos—an ethos that moulds and modifies the consciousness of an individual.

Desire for freedom, loyalty towards tradition, attraction towards modernity and change are the themes in all her novels. Her characters are found oscillating between the need of freedom from traditional restrictions and social obligations. The author has faithfully presented the changing attitudes of her characters for adopting a new way of life, searching for an escape from social taboos. Her characters also want to accept their responsibilities towards society. But for true and positive freedom does not mean the outright rejection of social duties, obligations and functions.

Kamala Markandaya is an ardent believer in mutual love and understanding. She tries her best to bring together the people of two diverse races and two different attitudes of life. The juxtaposition and interaction of two different civilizations, the Eastern and the Western, are very minutely discussed by the novelist, because her own personality combines in itself the antipodal values of two cultures. She is always in favour of cultural synthesis and compromise between the two ways of life. A peaceful and happy relationship can be developed only by mutual understanding, appreciation and respect. Markandaya claims that the meeting of the twain—the East and the West, is always possible at least, on the personal level, as it is evident in the relationship of Rukmani and Kenny in *Nectar in a Sieve,* the Mira-Richard relationship in *Some Inner Fury,* Vale-Ellie in *Possession,* Helen-Bashiam in *The Coffer Dams*, Srinivas-Mrs. Pickering and Srinivas and Rikki-Tully in *Pleasure City* despite the social, economical, political and cultural differences between the two races. As a keen observer, Markandaya investigates the merits and demerits of both the cultures neutrally. She highlights the economic backwardness, fatalism and passive endurance of the nation despite her traditional, philosophical, religious and ethical values. She appreciates and acknowledges the scientific and technological advancement of the West although it is heartless and soulless. She believes that India and Britain can only live in amity if they respect each other's sovereignty and effect a reconciliation in the spirit of 'forgive and forget'.

Markandaya has made her fiction a forum for her sensitive cry against suffering caused by recial discrimination. She is aware of the problem of the ruler and the ruled. Still she is in favour of universal equality all the time.

Other major inputs of her fiction are hunger and poverty, racial distinction and cultural crisis. She brilliantly portrays in the prevailing cultural millieu of modern India, the pleasures and pains of the rapidly changing society and the relief born out of the cultural continuty.

Markandaya's tour de force, *Nectar in a Sieve,* is a stark depiction of the Indian reality; it is an indictment of industrial economy, zamindari system, starvation and hunger. Dr. Kennington, representing the West, is a cultivated and enlightened British missionary and his heart is full of the milk of human kindness; and, hence, he has a strong sense of pity for the poor. He sacrifices his conjugal happiness for the welfare of the humanity. He works sincerely for the uplift of the downtrodden. He succeeds in curing Rukmani and her daughter, Ira, of their barrenners. Further, a hospital is built up by him for charity. The construction of the tannery introduces a new set of values. Rukmani reacts to the changing economic condition in her own life. Srinivas Iyengar suggests:

> One must hope, and one must persevere even if one is engaged only in trying to discover "nectar in a sieve".[1]

Tannery is a symbol of modernity. Its establishment is strongly opposed by Rukmani, but there is revelation of her mute acceptance of change and modernity. Indeed it shows human endurance. It is indeed a tribute to a woman of exemplary courage. Hence, the novel concentrates on the conflict between the traditional values of India and industrial and material values of the West. In *Some Inner Fury,* the East-West confrontation remains the predominant issue. It is an eloquent cry of despair. Between the two opposite forces of the East and the West, it is the story of love and death, awakening and sacrifice. Mirabai, a Western educated woman decides to join the nationalists without taking any heed of her British friend and lover, Richard. Her patriotism wins over her personal sentiments. The title is apt as it suggests the inner turmoil—Mira's emotional inner fury at the one hand and the country's political rage on the other.

A *Silence of Desire* is another powerful novel. It highlights the realm of spiritual realities. The significant issue of the society, the conflict between faith and rationalism, is the theme of this novel. The moral of the novel hinges on the scientific reality *vis-à-vis* religious faith. The Swamy, a spiritual figure, provides solace to the man who is in a deep worry. For Sarojini, the Swamy is an epitome of power, a silent power of faith:

> He is the silence—not of desire, fear or anger, but of a powerful personality, capable of

> inspiring thought in others without having recourse to speech.[2]

Socio-cultural economic conflict between the Eastern and the Western values is delineated in *Possession*, too. It is considered as a quest for identity, for spirituality, as against the worldly. The novel is a powerful exploration of the distortion of India's national character in the British fold and of her ultimate urge to be free. Valmiki represents India while Lady Caroline, stands for the British. Val undergoes a complete transformation under the influence of Caroline and acquires the manners and fashion of a well-bred Western young man.

In *A Handful of Rice*, Kamala Markandaya has based her theme of hunger and poverty, exodus from the village to the city and a search for identity that is lost forever in the impersonal atmosphere of the cities. Ravi, the protagonist, leaves his native village in order to get job in the city but he suffers a lot for criminal activities. Ravi's father and his father-in-law, Appu, follow the tradition without any ifs and buts but Ravi is pained to see that the value system and code of conduct of Appu are meaningless in the world of greed, dishonesty, and blackmarketing. Ravi is presented here as an angry protester.

In *The Coffer Dams,* there is a description of need to construct a forward-looking, industrialized India, at the national level; and the power of relationship between the two individuals of different backgrounds. The novel also discusses the themes of East-West encounter, man-woman relationship, the tension between technological power and nature and tradition and modernity. The novel deals with the problem of the English living in India and their relationship with the natives. The construction of dam is a symbol of scientific attitude that tries to over-power the natural course and flow of river. The novel is set in modern India but the conflict of values at its heart is universal.

The problem of an expatriate comes to light in *The Nowhere Man.* Srinivas, the central figure of the novel, feels alienated and utterly isolated in an adopted country, though he has a host of good friends. He is a victim of racial conflict. The theme of East-West encounter is very pervasive here. It is a novel of confrontation rather than of reconciliation.

The conflict between the old and the new, the tradition and the modernity and the rural and the urban ethos by juxtaposing the two different attitudes of the two sisters—Lalitha and Saroja is very excellently explored in *Two Virgins.* All the characters of this novel represent in varying degree—the traditional belief or the modern ways.

The Golden Honeycomb dramatises the individual desire for personal freedom in the absence of true political freedom. A vivid picture of the British Raj's dealings with the Indian Princes as well as their problems is presented here. The human relationship is pin-pointed very deeply. In this novel, Markandaya "opens up newer, mature frontiers by stressing the importance of filial and conjugal life."[3] The story is set in the state of Devapur and deals with the saga of almost a hundred years of Bawaji Raj family.

Pleasure City is an outstanding work of reconciliation between India and Britain. There is a complete lack of confrontation between the two. The Englishman exhibits a brilliant understanding and sensitivity to the spirit of India and her traditional values. The people of India here are ready to honour the benefits of modern technology.

Markandaya's latest novel, *The Catalyst: Alias Bombay Tiger*, published posthumously in 2007, is set in a landscape of the 1980s. The finished typescript of this unpublished novel was discovered shortly after her death by her daughter. The novel presents the story of Ganguli—mercurial, larger—than life—who arrives in Bombay with little more than ruthless ambition and finally becomes the biggest industrialist of the city. He is emblematic of a changing India, after the era of high socialism and he gets transformed by his private enterprise. The novel highlights his dramatic rise and fall, his loves and losses, and his eventual redemption. It is a remarkable novel revealing her profound feeling for humanity.

In this way, the whole discussion in the present work of mine is just a detached endeavour to present a description of inter-cultural relationship between the East and the West.

Preservation of tradition and acceptance of modernity are the prime objectives that seem to be best achieved in the fiction of Kamala Markandaya and a brilliant delineation of their mutual adaptibility has been focussed with full swing.

NOTES

1. K.S. Srinivas Iyengar, *Indian Writing in English*, Sterling Publishers Pvt. Ltd. New Delhi, 1985, p. 439.
2. Margaret P. Joseph, *Kamala Markandaya*, Arnold-Heinemann, New Delhi, 1980, p. 37.
3. Shantha Krishnaswamy, *The Woman in Indian Fiction in English, 1950-80*, Ashish Publishing House, New Delhi, 1984, p. 229.

Bibliography

PRIMARY SOURCES

A. Novels

Markandaya, Kamala. *Nectar in a Sieve.* Mumbai: Jaico Publishing House, 2003.

——*Some Inner Fury,* London: Putnam, 1955.

——*A Silence of Desire,* New Delhi: Hind Pocket Books, 1965.

——*Possession,* Bombay: Jaico Publishing House, 1994.

——*A Handful of Rice,* New Delhi: Orient Paperbacks, 1985.

——*The Coffer Dams,* New Delhi: Penguin Books India Pvt. Ltd., 2008.

——*The Nowhere Man,* Bombay: Orient Longman, 1975.

——*Two Virgins,* New Delhi: Vikash Publishing House, 1977.

——*The Golden Honeycomb,* London: Chatto and Windus, 1977.

——*Pleasure City,* London: Chatto and Windus, 1982.

——*Bombay Tiger,* New Delhi: Penguin Books India Pvt. Ltd., 2008.

B. Articles and Essays

Markandaya, Kamala. "One Pair of Eyes: Some Random Reflections." Lecture Addressed to European Branch of ACLALS in Stirling, Scotland, 1st Week of April, 1965. *The Literary Criterion,* 11, 4 (Summer 1975), 13-25.

——*"On Images",* Paper Read at the Seminar in Socio-Literature at the East-West Centre for Cultural Interchange, Honolulu, Aug., 1973.

——*"Why Do We Write in English",* Adam, Nos. 355-60(1971), pp. 42-43.

SECONDARY SOURCES

A. Books

Abidi, S.H.Z., Kamala Markandaya's Nectar in a Sieve: A Critical Study, Bareilly: Prakash Book Depot, 1976.

Almeida, Rochelle. Originality and Imitation: Indianness in the Novels of Kamala Markandaya, New Delhi: Rawat, 2000.

Badal, R.K. *Kamala Markandaya,* Bareilly: Prakash Book Depot, 1973.

Banerji, Niroj. *Kamala Markandaya: A Critical Study,* Allahabad: Kitab Mahal, 1990.

Bhatnagar, M.K. *Kamala Markandaya, A Critical Spectrum,* New Delhi: Atlantic Publishers and Distributors, 2002.

Chadha, Ramesh. *Cross-Cultural Interaction in Indian English Fiction: An Analysis of the Novels of Ruth Jhabvala and Kamala Markandaya,* New Delhi: National Book Organisation, 1988.

Das, B.K. *Kamala Markandaya's A Handful of Rice: A Critical Study*. Bareilly: Prakash Book Depot, N.D.

Dhawan, R.K. (ed), *Indian Women Novelists: Kamala Markandaya,* Set II: Vols. II and III. New Delhi: Prestige Publishers, 1993.

Garg, Neeraj. *Kamala Markandaya's Vision of Life,* New Delhi, Sarup and Sons, 2003.

Jha, Rekha. The Novels of Kamala Markandaya, Ruth Jhabvala: A Study in East-West Encounter. New Delhi: Prestige Books, 1990.

Joseph, M.P. *Kamala Markandaya,* New Delhi: Arnold-Heinemann, 1980.

Kalinnikova, Elena J. *Indian English Literature: A Perspective,* Ghaziabad: Vimal Prakashan, 1982.

Misra, Pravati. Class Consciousness in the Novels of Kamala Markandaya, New Delhi: Atlantic, 2001.

Parameshwaran Uma. *Writers of the Indian Diaspora, Kamala Markandaya,* New Delhi: Rawat Publication, 2000.

Pathania, Usha. Human Bonds and Bondages: The Fiction of Anita Desai and Kamala Markandaya, Delhi: Kanishka Publishing House, 1992.

Piciucco, Pier Paolo (ed), *A Companion to Indian Fiction in English*, New Delhi: Atlantic Publication, 2004.

Prasad, Amar Nath (ed), *Indian Writing in English: Critical Explorations*, New Delhi: Sarup & Sons, 2002.

Prasad, H.M. (ed), *Response: Recent Revelations of Indian Fiction in English*, Bareilly: Prakash Book Depot, 1983.

Prasad, Madhusudan (ed), *Perspectives on Kamala Markandaya*, Ghaziabad: Vimal Prakashan, 1984.

Raizada, Harish. *Indian English Novelists: Some Points of View*, Delhi: K.K. Publications, 1996.

Rao, A.V. Krishna and Menon Madhavi. *Kamala Markandaya: A Critical Study of Her Novels, 1954-1982*, Delhi: B.R. Publishing Corporation, 1997.

Reddy, K. Venkata. *Major Indian Novelists*, New Delhi: Prestige Books, 1990.

Roy, Mohit K. and Kundu Rama (ed). *Studies in Women Writers in English*, 4 volumes, New Delhi: Atlantic, 2004.

Rubin, David. *After the Raj : British Novels of India since 1947*, New England, Hanover and London: University Press, 1986.

Singh, Nagendra Kumar. Society and Self in the Novels of Ruth P. Jhabvala and Kamala Markandaya, New Delhi: Sarup and Sons, 2005.

Srivastava, R.K. *The Novels of Kamala Markandaya: A Critical Study*, Amritsar: Guru Nanak Dev University, 1998.

Wali, S.K. Kamala Markandaya: Nectar in a Sieve: A Stylistic Study, Jaipur: Printwell Publishers, 1987.

B. Articles

Adkins, Joan F. "Kamala Markandaya: Indo-Anglian Conflict as Unity." *Journal of S. Asian Literature,* 10, 1 (Fall 1974).

Ahmed, Hema. "Kamala Markandaya and the Indian Immigrant Experience in Britain." *Reworlding: The Literature of the Indian Diaspora.* Ed. Emmanuel S. Nelson, Westport: C.T. Greenwood, 1992.

Aithal, S.K. "Of the Bone and the Flesh: Kamala Markandaya's *Possession.*" *Journal of Literary Studies*, 4, 2 (Dec. 1981).

Appasamy, S.P. "*The Golden Honeycomb:* A Saga of Princely India by Kamala Markandaya, *The Journal of Indian Writing in English*, 6.2 (July 1978).

Asnani, Shyam M. "East and West Encounter in Kamala Markandaya's Later Novels", *Triveni,* 48, 4 (Jan.-March, 1980).

Argyle, Berry, "Kamala Markandaya's *Nectar in a Sieve,*" *Ariel,* 14.1 (1973).

Bande, Usha. "Beyond Culture: A Study of Kamala Markandaya's *Possession.*" *Manascarya: An International Journal of Cultural Studies* 4-53 (1998)

Barche, G.D. "Inside the Haveli and *The Nowhere Man*: A Study in Upanishadic Principle." *Psychic Knot: Search for Tolerance in Indian English Fiction.* New Delhi: Bahri Publications, 1998.

Chandrashekharan, K.R. "East and West in the Novels of Kamala Markandaya." *Critical Essays on Indian Writing in English.* Eds. M.K. Naik et al. Dharwar: Karnatak University Press, 1968.

Chari, Venkata K. "Kamala Markandaya's *Nectar in a Sieve:* A Study in Romantic Realism." *Kakatiya Journal of English Studies,* 3, 1 (1978).

——."Sense of Life in Kamala Markandaya's *Nectar in a Sieve*", *Osmania Journal of English Studies,* No. 9 (1972).

Chauhan, P.S. "Kamala Markandaya: Sense and Sensibility." *Literary Criterion,* 12, 2-3 (1976).

Dash, Parvati, "Women Characters in the Novels of Kamala Markandaya." *The Mahanadi Review* 2, No. 4.

Dunn, T.A. "Intensity and Crispness." *Journal of Commonwealth Literature,* No. 5 (July 1968).

Eliot, T.S. *Selected Poems,* Faber and Faber, London, 1976.

Geetha, P. "Kamala Markandaya's Novels—An Interpretation." *Commonwealth Quarterly* 3.9 (Dec. 1978).

Gooneratne, Y. "Traditional Elements in the Fiction of Kamala Markandaya, R.K. Narayan, and R.P. Jhabvala" *WLWE,* 15, 1 (April 1976).

Harrex, S.C. "A Sense of Identity: The Novels of Kamala Markandaya." *Journal of Commonwealth Literature,* 6, 1 (1971).

——"The Fire and the Offering"; *The English Language Novel of India 1935-1970,* Vol. I Calcutta: Writers' Workshop, 1977.

Horst, Mary Hooper. "Kamala Markandaya." *New Circle 18.7* (March 1973).

Iredale, Rogar. "Society and Self-Knowledge in the Novels of Kamala Markandaya", *Tenor,* No. 2, Jan. 1979.

Iyer, Sudha R. "The Need for Tolerance: A Study of Kamala Markandaya." *Psychic Knot: Search for Tolerance in Indian English Fiction.* New Delhi, Bahri Publications, 1998. Jain, Jasbir. "The Novels of Kamala Markandaya." *Indian Literature,* 18.2 (April-June 1975).

Katamble, V.D. "*The Coffer Dams*: An Apology for Techno-industrialisation of Rural India" (Vortex Incorp. Probitas), I (Oct. 1979).

Krupaka, B. "Race Relations and *The Nowhere Man.*" *Literary Endeavour,* 2, Nos. 2 and 3.

Kumar, Shiv. K. "Tradition and Change in the Novels of Kamala Markandaya." *Osmania Journal of English Studies,* 7, No. 1 (1969).

Mahle, H.S. "Kamala Markandaya: East-West Passage." Ed. H.S. Mahle, *Indo-Anglian Fiction: Some Perceptions.* New Delhi: Jainsons Publications, 1988.

Mehta, P.P. "Kamala Markandaya." *Indo-Anglian Fiction: An Assessment.* 2nd ed. Bareilly: Prakash Book Depot, 1979.

Montgomery, Ruth. "Kamala Markandaya's *Nectar in a Sieve.*" *Wilson Library Bulletin,* 28 (Nov. 1963).

Mukherjee, Meenakshi. "Four Indo-Anglian Novels." *Miscellany,* No. 39 (June 1970).

——"The Theme of Displacement in Anita Desai and Kamala Markandaya." *WLWE,* 17, 1 (April 1978).

Parameswaran, Uma. "India for the Western Readers: A Study of Kamala Markandaya's Novels." *Texas Quarterly,* 10.2 (Summer 1968).

Prasad, Hari Mohan. "The Quintessence of Kamala Markandaya's Art." *Commonwealth Quarterly,* 3.9 (Dec. 1978).

Ramamurti, K.S. "Kamala Markandaya's *Two Virgins:* A Problem Novel," *Littcrit,* 7, 2 (Dec. 1981).

Rao, A.V.K. "Kamala Markandaya and the Novel of Sensibility." *The Indo-Anglian Novel and the Changing Tradition: A Study of the Novels of M.R. Anand, Kamala Markandaya, R.K. Narayan and Raja Rao,* 1930-65. Mysore: Rao and Raghavan, 1972.

——"The Golden Honeycomb: A Brief Study." *Studies in Indian Fiction in English.* Ed. G.S.B. Gupta, Gulbarga: JIWE Publications, 1987.

——"Continuity and Change in the Novels of Kamala Markandaya." ed. Madhusudan Prasad, *Perspectives of Kamala Markandaya.* Ghaziabad: Vimal Prakashan, 1984.

——"The Novels of Kamala Markandaya." *Studies in Contemporary Indian Fiction in English: A Study.* Ed. A.N. Dwivedi, New Delhi: Kitab Mahal, 1987.

——"Feminine Sensibility in Indo-Anglian Fiction." *Triveni,* 35, 4 (Jan. 1967).

Rao, K.S. Narayana. "Kamala Markandaya: The Novelist as Craftsman." *Indian Writing Today*, 3, 2 (April-June 1969).

——"Markandaya's *Possession* and the Idea of the Triumph of the Spirit: I." *The Indian P.E.N.*, 36, 10.

——"Markandaya's *Possession* and the Idea of the Triumph of the Spirit: II." *The Indian P.E.N.* 36, No. 11.

——"Novels of Kamala Markandaya," *Literature East and West*, 15, 2.

——"Religious Elements in Kamala Markandaya's Novels." *Ariel: A Review of International English Literature*, 8, I (Jan. 1977).

——"Some Notes on the Plots of Kamala Markandaya." *Indian Literature*, 13, 1 (March, 1970).

Rao, Vimala. "Indian Expatriates." "*The Journal of Commonwealth* Literature 10.3 (April 1976).

Roudiczek Raul, *Existentialism:* For and Against, London: Cambridge University Press, 1964 Sethuraman, R. "Writing Across Cultures: Sexual/Racial 'Othering' in Kamala Markandaya's *Possession*." *Ariel* 23, 3 (1992 July).

Sharma, Krishna S. "Two Recent Novels of Kamala Markandaya", *Triveni*, Vol. XLV, October-December 1976.

Singh, R.S. "Soulful East and Ratiocinative West—Kamala Markandaya." *Indian Novel in English: A Critical Study.* New Delhi: Arnold-Heinemann, 1977.

Srivastava, Ramesh K. "Clinton-Helen-Bashiam Relationship in Markandaya's *The Coffer Dams*." *Panjab Journal of English Studies*, 8 (1993).

——*Six Indian Novelist in English*, Amritsar: Guru Nanak Dev University Press, 1987.

Thakur, Guruprasad. "And Never the Twain Shall Meet—Kamala Markandaya's *Nowhere Man*." *Explorations in Modern Indo-English Fiction*. R.K. Dhawan (ed), New Delhi: Bahri Publications, 1982.

Thumboo, Edwin. "Kamala Markandaya's *A. Silence of Desire.*" *Journal of Indian Writing in English*, 8, 1-2 (Jan.-July 1980).

Venkateshwaran, Shyamala. "The Language of Kamala Markandaya's Novels." *The Literary Criterion,* 9.3 (Winter 1970).

Venugopal, C.V. "Kamala Markandaya's *Possession:* A Study." *Journal of the Karnataka Univ.,* 24 and 25 (1980-81).

Walsh, William. "Kamala Markandaya." *Contemporary Novelists.* Ed. James Vinson, 2nd Ed. New York: St. Martin's Press, 1976.

Weir, Ann Lowry. "Review of *The Nowhere Man* and Jai Nimbkar's *Temporary Answers. Journal of South Asian Literature*, 16, 1 (Spring 1981).

C. Other General Works

Badal, R.K. *Indo-Anglian Literature: An Outline.* Bareilly: Prakash Book Depot, 1975.

Bhakhtiyar, I. (ed.), *The Novel in Modern India:* Bombay: P.E.N. Centre, 1964.

Boulton, Marjorie. *The Anatomy of the Novel.* London: Routledge and Kegan Paul, 1975.

Britannica Ready Reference Encyclopedia, Vol. III, New Delhi.

Buck, Pearl, S. *The Good Earth* 1931; rpt. New York: New York Pocket Books, 1968.

Booth, Wayne C. *The Rhetoric of Fiction.* Chicago: Univ. of Chicago Press, 1961.

Caserio, R.L. *Plot, Story and the Novel,* Princeton: Univ. of Princeton Press, 1979.

Coomaraswamy, Ananda K. *The Dance of Shiva: Fourteen Indian Essays.* New Delhi: Sagar Publications, 1976

Eliot, T.S. *Selected Prose,* Great Britain: Penguin, 1958.

——Selected Poems, London: Faber and Faber, 1976.

"From Chatterjee to Chatterjee", *Indian Literature,* No. 144, July-August 1991.

Forster, E.M. *Aspects of the Novel.* London: Edward Arnold, 1927.

Greenberger, J. Allen. *The British Image of India*, London, 1969.

Haksar, Urmila. *The Future That Was.* Bombay Allied, 1972.

Harvey, W.J. *Character and the Novel.* London: Chatto and Windus, 1965.

Hemenway, S.I. *The Novel of India,* Vol. I: The *Anglo-Indian Novel.* Vol. 2: *The Indo-Anglian Novel.* Calcutta: Writers Workshop, 1975.

Hewitt, D. *The Approach to Fiction: Good and Bad Readings of Novels.* London: Longman, 1972.

——*I am the People*, New Delhi: NCERT, 2007.

Iyengar, K.R.S. and Kumar Prema Nand. *Indian Writing in English*, 4th Ed., New Delhi: Sterling, 1984.

——*Indian Writing in English*, New Delhi: Sterling, 1985.

Joseph, S. John Peter. "Confrontation and Reconciliation in the Novels of Kamala Markandaya", *Studies in Women Writers in English*, Vol. I (ed.) Mohit K. Roy and Rama Kundu, New Delhi: Atlantic, 2004.

Krishnaswamy, Shantha. *The Woman in Indian Fiction in English, 1950-80,* New Delhi: Ashish Publishing House, 1984.

"Markandaya Kamala (1924) Indian Novelist", *Encyclopedia of Post-Colonial Literatures in English* (ed.) Eugene Beson and L.W. Conolly, Vol. 2, London: Routledge, 1994.

Masters John. *The Night Runners of Bengal*, New York, 1951.

Modern Essays, Orient Longman, 2001.

Mukherjee, M. *The Twice-Born Fiction.* New Delhi: Arnold-Heinemann, 1973.

Naik, M.K. *A History of Indian English Literature.* New Delhi: Sahitya Akademi, 1982.

Naik, M.K. et al. *Critical Essays on Indian Writing in English.* Dharwar: Karnataka Univ. Press, 1972.

Nanda Kumar Prema. *Indian Writing in English*, Three Cheers, Indian Literature, Volume XIII, No. 4, 1970.

Narasimhaiah, C.D. *The Swan and the Eagle.* Simla: I.I.A.S., 1969.

Parameswaran, Uma. A Study of Representative Indo-English Novelists, New Delhi: Vikas, 1976.

Pink, M.A. *Points of View*, Macmillan, 1975.

Prose and Poetry Selections, Patna: Sunrise Publication, 1996.

Reddy, G.A. *Indian Writing in English and Its Audience.* Bareily: Prakash Book Depot, 1979.

Shirwadkar, Meena. *Image of Woman in the Indo-Anglian Novel.* New Delhi: Sterling, 1979.

Singer, Milton. (ed.), *Introducing Indian Liberal Education*, Chicago, 1957.

Singh, Bhupal. *A Survey of Ango Indian Fiction*, London: Curzon Press, 1934.

Srivastava, A.K. (ed.), *Alien Voice*, Lucknow: Print House, 1981.

Steel. The Hosts of the Lord, New Delhi.

Trilling, Lionel. *Beyond Culture.* London: Secker and Warburg, 1966.

Walsh, William. *Commonwealth Literature.* London: O.U.P., 1973.

Readings in *Commonwealth Literature.* London: Clarendon Press, 1973.

Williams, H.M. "Indo-Anglian Literature (1800-1970): A Survey". Madras: Orient Longman, 1976. *Studies in Modern Indian.*

Fiction in English. Calcutta: Writers Workshop, 1973.

D. Online Materials

Assisi, C. Francis. "Homage to Kamala Markandaya." Online: http.//www.beilharz.com/authors/markandaya. Accessed on 3/31/2007.

Chambers, Claire, Leads Metropolitan University. "Kamala Markandaya". *The Literary Encyclopedia, Online:* http: www.litencyc.com/php/speople.php?rec=true & UID = 2936, Accessed on 4/2/2007.

Kohli Suresh. Society, "She took India to the US". Online: http://www.boloji.com/wfs252.htm. Accessed on 4/2/2007.

Parmeswaran Uma. "Kamala Markandaya". Online http://www.sawnet.org/books/authors.php? Markandaya + Kamala. Accessed on 3/31/2007.